SELECTED POEMS

JOHN GAY was born in 1685 in Barnstaple, Devon, and educated at Barnstaple Grammar School. In 1702 he was apprenticed to a silk mercer in London, although he never completed his apprenticeship. He began to write pamphlets and broadsheets, and to mix in literary circles. From 1712 to 1714 Gay was domestic steward to the Duchess of Monmouth. The dedication of his *Rural Sports* in 1713 to Alexander Pope led to their friendship, and at Pope's instigation Gay published *The Shepherd's Week* in 1714. In the same year he was appointed secretary to Lord Clarendon, ambassador to the court of Hanover. In 1720 Gay published *Poems on Several Occasions* by subscription, but the profits that the volume made him were lost in the South Sea Bubble speculation. Gay continued to search for preferment at court, supported by his literary friends. He was made Commissioner for the State Lottery in 1723, and was offered, and refused, the post of gentleman usher to Princess Louisa in 1727. *The Beggar's Opera* (1728) a satire on the corruption of society, recouped Gay's fortunes, although the production of its sequel was banned. In 1729 Gay went to live in the house of the Duchess of Queensberry, whose patronage continued until his death in 1732.

MARCUS WALSH is Professor of English Literature at the University of Birmingham. The author of many studies of eighteenth-century writing, he has a particular interest in the works of Gay's contemporaries, Swift, Pope, Johnson, Sterne and Smart. He has edited a selection of the religious poetry of Christopher Smart for the Fyfield series.

Fyfield*Books* aim to make available some of the great classics of British and European literature in clear, affordable formats, and to restore often neglected writers to their place in literary tradition.

Fyfield*Books* take their name from the Fyfield elm in Matthew Arnold's 'Scholar Gypsy' and 'Thyrsis'. The tree stood not far from the village where the series was originally devised in 1971.

> *Roam on! The light we sought is shining still.*
> *Dost thou ask proof? Our tree yet crowns the hill,*
> *Our Scholar travels yet the loved hill-side*

from 'Thyrsis'

JOHN GAY

Selected Poems

Edited with an introduction by
MARCUS WALSH

FyfieldBooks

CARCANET

First published in Great Britain in 1997 by
Carcanet Press Limited
Alliance House
Cross Street
Manchester M2 7AQ

This impression 2003

A CIP catalogue record for this book is available from the British Library
ISBN 1 85754 702 0

The publisher acknowledges financial assistance from
the Arts Council of England

Printed and bound in England by SRP Ltd, Exeter

CONTENTS

INTRODUCTION

CLOSE contemporary and friend of Pope and Swift, John Gay has almost always been seen in their shadow. Samuel Johnson in his *Life* of Gay, written nearly fifty years after Gay's death, described him as 'a play-fellow rather than a partner' in the 'association of wits', and this assessment has been an unconscionable time dying. Gay is known chiefly for his most obvious and lasting success, *The Beggar's Opera*; his extensive and excellent non-dramatic poetry, with the exception of the first volume of the *Fables*, has not had so wide a following, and only recently have critics felt able to make appropriately large claims for it. It is the purpose of this selection to make Gay the poet more available, and of this Introduction to suggest what kind of claims can be made.

Gay is an ironist rather than a satirist; he has suffered unfairly in reputation for his lack of the distinctively satiric qualities of his great contemporaries. If we are looking for the high seriousness which (*pace* Matthew Arnold) we now find in the poetry of Pope, for the moral indignation that arises from idealism, we shall be disappointed. Pope has a large and apprehensible vision of the good society and the good man, though he portrays them at least as often by their negatives as by their positives. Gay, the laughing philosopher, has a realist's sense of the universal fallibility of man, and rarely allows his reader the luxury of reposing upon an absolute value. Pope uses satiric *personae*, the virtuous friend and pious son of the *Epistle to Arbuthnot*, the embattled defender of public virtue of the *Epilogue to the Satires*, but these *personae* are recognisable, stable within their contexts, and give relatively clear moral guidance. Gay often uses the first person (as in *Trivia*), or even his own name (as in the Proeme to the *Shepherd's Week*), but we can rarely be sure how this authorial voice is to be taken. His works contain political and social satire, but he seldom identifies his target with a satirist's certainty. Gay does not have the heroic intellectual and moral vision of Pope, and his ironist's taste for observing life from the fence deprives much of his poetry of the highest commitment.

Yet if Gay's work does not have the qualities of great satire, it offers ample compensating values proper to its own rather different kind. Gay is the most acute observer of human life, always ready to be amused by, and to record with a deadly verbal suggestiveness, the real motives that lie hidden behind pretence, to catch exactly the ambivalent tones of human intercourse. His chosen weapon is literary adaptation; he is one of the foremost masters in English of parody, burlesque and pastiche, constantly testing the assumptions of literary conventions against the many sharp edges of actual experience. One of the great virtues and pleasures of Gay's poetry is its sense of verbal and formal play. This element of literary exercise is not mere self-indulgence; rather it makes possible a detached, sober and often de-lighted appreciation of life as it is.

Wine, the first poem in this selection, is an early essay in a relatively minor literary mode, following the example set by John Philips in *The Splendid Shilling* (1701) of applying to a common subject an elevated, Miltonic, poetic idiom. Johnson suggests in his *Life* of Philips that 'the merit of such performances begins and ends with the first author', but Gay's repetition of the joke has some features of its own. The burlesque of Miltonic diction, syntax and imagery are turned to wryly suggestive purposes. Where Milton's epic in-vocation speaks of 'man's first disobedience, and the fruit / Of that forbidden tree', Gay introduces wine as 'the Source / Whence human pleasures flow'. The name of the tavern is the 'Devil Young or Old'; the 'Majestic Dame' is a perversion of the 'lowliness majestic' of the unfallen Eve; the sleepy tapster 'stumbles . . . / Erroneous'. These (and other) evocations of the Fall need not be taken too seriously; Gay reaches a typically practical compromise with wine, his charac-ters finding in it a relief from the self-indulgent melancholy, the 'pensive Hypoish Mood', which arises from the comically-viewed sorrows of marriage, pecuniary loss, or amorous disappointment. Notably wine enables Strephon to overcome his romantic ineffect-iveness, and win the 'Breach' by force. Drunkenness in moderation, it seems, may be a capital thing.

The derivations and purposes of *The Shepherd's Week* are complex. In 1709 pastorals by both Alexander Pope and Ambrose Philips appeared in Tonson's *Poetical Miscellanies*. Pope at first admired Philips' pastorals, but a campaign of justification and advertisement of Philips by members of the literary clique associated with Button's coffee house, and Pope's rapidly increasing alienation from this basically Whig group, caused him to mount a stinging ironic attack on Philips in *Guardian* 40 (1713). A letter from Pope to John Caryll of 8 June 1714 implied that Gay's *Shepherd's Week* was aimed at Philips and was connected with this quarrel.

The argument centred, insofar as it was not a matter of personalities, around the literary question of imitation. Does the pastoral poet (and of course there are implications beyond pastoral) imitate the actual and imperfect world, or does he rather offer an idealising imitation of perfected nature? Is he to write as Theocritus, Spenser and now Ambrose Philips do about more or less real rustics in a more or less realistic dialect, or should he, as Pope claims to, follow Virgil and write of an imagined Golden Age, in a more elegant, 'courtly' style?

Gay's *Shepherd's Week* may certainly be read as an attack on Philips. Hoyt Trowbridge has demonstrated in detail how Gay parodies Philips' obsolete language, simplicities of expression, rustic names, violations of decorum and platitudinous proverbs. In the Proeme, which itself borrows in word and phrasing from Philips' Preface, Gay announces his intention of providing realistic pastoral such 'as Nature in the Country affordeth'. A basic technique is reduction, modifying forms and words of Virgil's *Eclogues* according to the Philips formula as it was conceived, or intentionally misconceived, by Pope and Gay. We may see this illustrated by Gay's quotation, in his own note for 'Monday' 83, of his source passage in Virgil.

The Shepherd's Week however has a number of other targets. Tom D'Urfey the balladeer and song-writer, mentioned in 'Wednesday' and implied in the list of popular ballads in 'Saturday', is an example for Gay, as he seems to have been for Pope in *Guardian* 40, of the kind of poetry with which Philips' brand of pastoral might be compared. Addison, who had sponsored the popular ballads *Chevy-Chase* and *The Two Children in the Wood* in the *Spectator* (70, 74 and 85), is also a mark in 'Saturday'. If Gay's 'Doric' language echoes Philips, it also burlesques Spenser's far more archaic dialect in *The Shepheardes Calender*. As the Proeme makes clear *The Shepherd's Week* is in imitation of Spenser a (diminished) pastoral calendar. The Proeme is written in Gay's version of Elizabethan prose, and the footnotes (of

which I have printed those for 'Monday' as a sample) make fun of
E.K.'s original glosses to Spenser. Written at the height of the activities
of the Scriblerus Club, this poem is, with its elaborate apparatus, also
a wider and typically Scriblerian attack on the intrusion into humane
letters of a kind of false learning, that dull archaising pedantry to be
satirised by Pope under the name of Wormius:

'But who is he, in closet close y-pent,
Of sober face, with learned dust besprent?
Right well mine eyes arede the myster wight,
On parchment scraps y-fed, and Wormius hight.
To future ages may thy dulness last,
As thou preserv'st the dulness of the past!'

(*Dunciad Variorum* 3.181-86)

However, Gay is by no means toeing Pope's party line on pastoral,
but offering his own searching re-assessment of the genre. He rejects
not only the rustic of Spenser and the sentimentalised realism which
(rather than an exaggerated Doric) is characteristic of Philips, but also
the idealism of Pope. Gay here creates not merely academic parody,
but a new version of the convention itself, a pastoral of comic realism
with its own life independent of the quarrel that gave it birth. To use
the words of Samuel Johnson, who had a proper contempt for merely
artificial pastoral:

the effect of reality and truth became conspicuous . . . These
Pastorals became popular, and were read with delight, as just
representations of rural manners and occupations, by those who
had no interest in the rivalry of the poets, nor knowledge of
the critical dispute.

Labour and sexual love are viewed without rose-tinted lenses. Philips'
shepherds have an improbable delicacy:

In Summer Shade, beneath the cocking Hay,
What soft, endearing Words did she not say?
Her lap, with Apron deck'd, she kindly spread,
And stroak'd my Cheeks, and lull'd my leaning Head.

(6.57-60)

Gay's shepherds are altogether more cheerfully realistic:

As Blouzelinda in a gamesome Mood,
Behind a Haycock loudly laughing stood,
I slily ran, and snatch'd a hasty Kiss,
She wip'd her Lips, nor took it much amiss.

('Monday' 71-74)

Cloddipole reminds Lobbin and Cuddy that while they engage in a literary contest their herds are thirsty. 'Wednesday' would be a more romantic story of blighted love if Sparabella killed herself; more sensibly she concludes that most forms of death are attended by some inconvenience. In 'Saturday' the semi-divine Silenus of Virgil's sixth *Eclogue* is replaced by the country drunkard Bowzybeus, who informs his hearers not of 'the secret seeds of nature's frame' but, perhaps more usefully, of turnips and pick-pockets.

Trivia has reasonably been described, by William Irving in his biography of Gay, as 'without question the greatest poem on London life in English literature'. Juvenal's third *Satire*, on the dangers of life in Rome, is an obvious prototype, which had already been imitated by John Oldham (in his *Poems, and Translations*, 1683), and was to serve as the basis for Samuel Johnson's first major published poem, *London* (1738). Gay's energetic descriptions of streets jammed with carts, of the walker fighting his way in the crush, of the wealthy dame's coach attended by lines of flambeaux, are indebted to passages in Juvenal's classic evocation of urban chaos, though the *saeva indignatio* of the Roman satirist is not a feature of *Trivia*. Gay also owed 'several Hints' for his poem to two fragmentary satiric pieces by Swift, 'A Description of the Morning' (1709) and 'A Description of a City Shower' (1710), in which some of the more sordid details of city life are presented in an elevated heroic couplet verse.

The major literary example, however, for both Gay and Swift, is Virgil's *Georgics*. Whereas Swift in his limited compass parodies a few features, Gay produces a full-scale mock-georgic. In the four books of the *Georgics*, Virgil applies a high style to a low subject, diversifying extensive practical advice about farming with moral, mythological and historical digressions, and with praise of the Emperor Augustus, of Augustan Rome, of Augustan Italy, and of Augustan empire. Virgil's vision is of man at peace and a part of his country environment. In its claim to offer instruction, its elevated expression, its digressions and division into books, *Trivia* is a georgic. At many places the debt to Virgil, or to Dryden's translation of Virgil, is close, and signposted. Gay's lines on the 'Prognosticks' of the weather, for example, like those in Swift's 'A Description of a City Shower', follow a passage in the first *Georgic*, and Gay's repetition of 'certain Signs' is meant to point to Dryden's use of this phrase.

But Gay's employment of his Augustan model is in many ways ironic. Rural harmony has become urban discord. The praise of London as 'Happy Augusta! Law-defended Town' (3.145), a note of patriotism proper to the georgic mode, can scarcely be taken at face value in this context of theft, deceit, dangerous energy. All around are images of confusion, puzzle, violence: winding alleys, perplexing lanes, suffocating mists, tumultuous crowds, twirling turnstiles, mazy courts, dark abodes, guileful paths. The frequently-introduced comparisons with classic legend underline the discrepancy between the heroic aspirations of the georgic as a form, and the London world Gay is portraying. Trapped in mid-street between passing carts and coaches the walker becomes the mariner caught between Scylla and Charybdis, failing to avoid a quarrel he is reminded of the story of Oedipus.

There are points in *Trivia* at which the reader is offered, and may be tempted gratefully to accept, clear moral guidance. In this poem written for 'honest Men' (1.119) there is a frequent contrast between the virtuous poverty of those who walk and the luxurious vanity of those who ride, between 'Use' and 'empty Show'. This apparently lies behind the descriptions of 'the Midnight Visits of the Dame', attended by 'a Train of Torches' (3.157-60), or of a gaudy funeral procession (3.225-36): 'Is all this Pomp for laying Dust to Dust?' But Gay is to be suspected when he comes bearing morals. The context and the triteness of this last line seem to deflate its seriousness. The comic diction and imagery of the passage on the 'hapless Swain' have a similar effect (3.285-306): 'Canst thou forgo Roast-Beef for nauseous Pills?'

Nothing about *Trivia* is straightforward, not even the title, which means primarily crossroads, but is also a Roman name for the goddess Hecate (though Gay purports to invoke a more innocent goddess of the streets), points to the threefold structure of the poem, suggests the medieval *trivium* of studies in grammar, logic and rhetoric, and implies trivial in the modern sense. The poem is 'spoken' by an authorial voice who on a number of occasions presents himself, and his experiences as a walker, in the first person, but who certainly cannot be identified with Gay. (Gay's correspondence with Swift reveals that Gay's taste, or lack of taste, for exercise was something of a private joke). Everywhere there is irony hiding in words. We have to be constantly alive to such puns as lurk in the 'Loves and Graces' on the gamester's chariot (1.116), or the 'aking Breast' of the romantically inattentive stroller (3.104). There is an ironic revaluation involved in the periphrasis by which a pickpocket is called a 'subtil Artist' (3.54), and a quiet suggestion of real motive in the description of the coming of Spring: 'The Seasons operate on every Breast; / 'Tis hence that Fawns are brisk, and Ladies drest' (1.151-52). Through the whole poem the reader must be as wary of verbal ambush as the walker of dead ends and Drury Lane.

'The Tea-Table' and 'The Birth of the Squire' are selected here from the four 'Eclogues' which Gay included among his *Poems on Several Occasions* (1720). In these works Gay is moving closer to satire, using the pastoral form to comment on aspects of contemporary society. In 'The Tea-Table' Gay looks at the fashionable feminine world of St. James, visits, tea and cards. The two speakers are engaged in a parody of the conventional pastoral song-contest, allowing Gay both to make a literary joke and to show his heroines talking to, but not listening to, each other. The contest of amatory eulogy has here turned into a contest of malicious gossip. Doris and Melanthe are themselves satirists, murdering in 'sly, polite, insinuating stile' (the words are Pope's, of Horace) the reputation of the absent Sylvia and Laura. Doris and Melanthe themselves exist, however, in a satiric frame. Gay undercuts everything they are to say in his opening paragraph, and exposes their hypocrisy in the conclusion.The ironies re-echo: Melanthe's description of Laura as a prude (lines 79-82) could be applied to herself. As in *The Shepherd's Week* and *Trivia*, forms and appearances are tested against the more useful values of real life, and positives emerge through double ironic layers:

> Cynthio can bow, takes snuff, and dances well,
> Robin talks common sense, can write and spell;

Sylvia's vain fancy dress and show admires,
But 'tis the man alone who Laura fires.

(lines 59-62)

'The Birth of the Squire' is a parody of a classic 'prophetic song', Virgil's fourth *Eclogue*. The satire is more direct, Gay dispensing here, unusually, with a *persona*. Virgil's poem had celebrated (it is thought) the birth of a child, Saloninus, the son of the Consul Pollio, and associated that birth with the coming of a new Golden Age. Where Saloninus restores innocence and security, in which the 'lowing herds secure from lions, feed', Gay's booby squire is the destructive hunter. Only when the squire's 'solid sense' and 'nod important' (phrases which look forward to the characteristic diction of Pope's *Dunciad*) are busied enforcing the law against poachers is the animal creation safe. Though the parody of Virgil is not sustained at the structural level, verbal echoes of Dryden's translation of the fourth *Eclogue* insist on the inversion of Virgilian values. The 'nauseous qualms' of the mother of Saloninus, for example, become the 'watry qualms' of the milkmaid the squire has seduced. That 'the dairy, barn, the hayloft and the grove / Shall oft' be conscious of their stolen love' recalls a more famous and heroic mating, that of Dido and Aeneas in the fourth Book of the *Aeneid*:

Hell from below, and Juno from above,
And howling Nymphs, were conscious to their Love.

(tr. Dryden 243-44)

Gay's *Fables*, and especially the first volume (1727), have been much the most popular of his poems. Among the numerous editions that have appeared between Gay's time and ours are those with illustrations by Thomas Bewick (1779) and William Blake (1793). Though there were few English precedents, Gay had ancient models in Aesop and the Roman Phaedrus, and a more recent major example in La Fontaine.

Gay's fables nonetheless are an original development of the genre. Johnson, with his usual sharp eye for 'compositions of a distinct kind', and his usual demand for the clear moral statement, nicely describes both the formal variety of Gay's fables, and their teasing ambiguity:

A Fable or Apologue . . . seems to be in its genuine state a narrative in which beings irrational, and sometimes inanimate . . . are for the purpose of moral instruction feigned to act and speak with human interests and passions. To this description the compositions of Gay do not always conform. For a Fable he gives now and then a Tale or an abstracted Allegory; and from some, by whatever name they may be called, it will be difficult to extract any moral principle.

Gay's animals do not always function as fable figures. Sometimes they are representatives of human types, sometimes they are clearly not human. There is no simple repetition of figurative procedure from one fable to the next, but a multiplicity of moral perspectives and tones. On the one hand, for example, we have the serious moral allegory of 'The Father and Jupiter' (*Fable* 39), a concise working of the theme Johnson was to use in *The Vanity of Human Wishes*; on the other the distinctly comic tale of 'The Fox at the Point of Death' (*Fable* 29). Often a fable presents us with a variety of targets. In 'The Elephant and the Bookseller' (*Fable* 10), for instance, Gay aims at dubious travel-books, the decline of learning, opportunist and ignorant booksellers, and the disputes of authors, as well as giving his somewhat absurd elephant the opportunity of mocking the human habit of making animals the types of all vices.

Despite Gay's usual ironic polyvalence, it may be possible to extract from his fables a 'moral principle'. Gay's chief and consistent concerns may be identified as vanity, the lack of self-knowledge, the mistaking of motive. In 'The Fox at the Point of Death' ideal morality is tried against the realities of self-interest. The dying fox, cultivating his conscience, and remembering the last Act of *Richard III*, sees the ghosts of murdered game; his healthy children look in vain for a square meal, and have little difficulty in persuading their sire to take a more reasonable attitude. The fable is an injunction not against theft and murder (once a fox, always a fox), but against unrealistic moral pretensions.

Moral blindness may sometimes be seen as the result of a failure to perceive one's correct place in the Chain of Being that stretches from God to the lowest creatures. Important to Gay here was the prevalent Augustan tendency to test man's moral behaviour for its propriety to his place in the Chain, and to image him as an animal of some kind where he fails. Pope's Sporus, in the *Epistle to Dr.Arbuthnot*, perverting beauty, parts, wit and pride, becomes a butterfly, a spaniel, a toad. And one thinks especially of Swift's impossible and inhuman extremes of rational horses and bestial apes in the fourth voyage of *Gulliver's Travels*. In such a context, the fable becomes a perfect form for the investigation of man's moral nature. Thus in *Fable* 40 two grave apes, imagining themselves, as mankind may do with a restricted vision, to be the prototypes of wisdom, are amused that men should apparently try to imitate their gymnastic skills, and themselves therefore become typical of those who will not allow the real value of others. The apes indeed are presented as fashionable human snobs, commenting on the gaping, draggled populace:

Brother, says Pug, and turn'd his head,
The rabble's monstrously ill-bred.

(lines 27-28)

Behind this is the serious philosophical question of man's paradoxical place in the Chain of Being between apes and angels, his 'strong reason' (to borrow the terminology of the elephant of *Fable* 10) poised between bestial instinct and angelic intuition. In calling mankind the 'giant apes of reason' Gay's apes are stating a truth similar to that more fully expressed by Pope in the *Essay on Man*:

Superior beings, when of late they saw
A mortal Man unfold all Nature's law,
Admir'd such wisdom in an earthly shape,
And shew'd a NEWTON as we shew an Ape.

(2.31-34)

In the last resort the vaunted abilities of the human race are as relative as the distinct qualities of scholar and fop, of *Don* and *Monsieur*, of poets and sons of prose.

In the *Fables* of 1727 there is often an element of satire at the expense of contemporary society. 'The Jugglers' (*Fable* 42) may be an allegory of vice, but the vices are given some of the clothes of Gay's time. The butterfly of *Fable* 24 may be taken as a newly-rich Whig gentleman. Nonetheless, in these earlier fables Gay preserves his characteristic stance of the disinterested ironist. There is no simple moral message, and no single satiric target. In the second volume of *Fables*, written in 1731-32 but not published until 1738, Gay becomes more openly a satirist and a moralist. It is appropriate that the mask used in the frontispiece of the 1727 volume has become in 1738 a portrait. *Fable* 1, in some ways like Pope's *First Satire of the Second Book of Horace Imitated* (1733), is an explicit apology for satire, announcing Gay's intention to 'lash vice in gen'ral fiction' (line 49) and hold up the glass of satire to mankind (line 54). The 1738 *Fables* are much more directly concerned with the actual political world. In *Fable* 2, for example, Gay contemplates from retirement the corruption of power, the conspicuous disclaimers of the preamble making it clear that these lines should be read as an attack on Robert Walpole's political methods. Gay goes beyond personalities, however, in the direction of wider moral statement, claiming to 'draw from gen'ral nature' (1.37) and speaking seriously of such large abstract concepts as 'virtue' (16. 149-54). His change of attitude is reflected in the changed, and more straightforward, structure of these later poems, in which the fable itself provides a more vivid illustrating image of a moral idea already rather fully stated in the long epistolary introduction. Composing these fables at the same time as Pope was at work on the *Epistles to Several Persons*, Gay finds in the verse-epistle a proper form for a poetry more overtly ethical than he had previously written.

The *Fables* of 1738 approach closer, then, to a method and tone of Pope, and reveal a darkening of political and moral vision in Gay comparable to that which marks Pope's great poetry of the later 1730s and the early 1740s, the Horatian imitations, the *Epilogue to the Satires*, the fourth Book of the *Dunciad*. The 1738 *Fables* represent a close to Gay's career, not only as the last work composed before his death, but as an indication that, in his search for greater weight and clarity of moral statement, he was prepared partly to sacrifice the fruitful detachment, the delicate ironic poise, which is the distinguishing note of his best work.

1685, June 30 Gay born in Barnstaple.

               Attends Barnstaple Grammar School.

c. 1702   Becomes apprentice to a silk-mercer in London.

1706   Released from articles; returns to Barnstaple.

1707   Returns to London. Becomes secretary to the journalist Aaron Hill.

1708   *Wine.*

1711   Begins his lasting friendship with Alexander Pope. Pamphlet and broadside writing while seeking preferment.

1712   *The Mohocks.*

1712-14   Domestic steward of Duchess of Monmouth.

1713   *The Wife of Bath* produced and published. *The Fan. Rural Sports.*

1714   *The Shepherd's Week. A Letter to a Lady.* Secretary of the Scriblerus Club. June-Sept., Secretary to Lord Clarendon on diplomatic mission to Hanover.

1715   *The What d'ye Call It* produced and published.

1716   *Trivia.*

1717   *Three Hours after Marriage* produced and published.

1720   *Poems on Several Occasions.* Loses the substantial profits from this volume in the South Sea Bubble.

1723   Becomes Commissioner of the State Lottery.

1724   *The Captives* produced and published.

1725   *To a Lady on her Passion for Old China.*

1727   *Fables*, first volume. The long quest for preferment culminates in the offer of the post of Gentleman Usher to Princess Louise, which Gay declines.

1728   *The Beggar's Opera* produced and published, recouping Gay's financial fortunes.

1729   *Polly*, the sequel to *The Beggar's Opera*, published, though its production is banned. Gay goes to live in the house of the Duchess of Queensberry, who had been banished from court for soliciting subscriptions for *Polly*.

1730	*The Wife of Bath* produced, published in revised form.
1731	*Acis and Galatea* produced, with music by Handel; the libretto is published alone the following year.
1732	Gay dies December 4.
1738	*Fables*, second volume.

SELECT BOOKLIST

The Poetical Works of John Gay. Ed. G. C. Faber. London, 1926.
John Gay: Poetry and Prose. Ed. V. A. Dearing and C. E. Beckwith: 2 vols. Oxford, 1974. Now the standard edition.
The Shepherd's Week. 1714. Facsimile edn. Menston, 1969.
Fables. 1727 and 1738. Facsimile edn. Menston, 1969.
The Letters of John Gay. Ed. C. F. Burgess. Oxford, 1966.

Samuel Johnson. Life of Gay in Johnson's *Lives of the English Poets*. Ed. G. Birkbeck Hill. 3 vols. Oxford, 1905.

C. F. Burgess. 'Scriblerian Influence in *The Shepherd's Week*'. *Notes and Queries* N. S. 10 (1963), 218.
J. Chalker. *The English Georgic*. London, 1969.
J. E. Congleton. *Theories of Pastoral Poetry in England 1684-1798*. Gainesville, 1952.
D. L. Durling. *Georgic Tradition in English Poetry*. New York, 1935.
W. D. Ellis Jr. 'Thomas D'Urfey, the Pope-Philips Quarrel, and *The Shepherd's Week*'. *Publications of the Modern Language Association of America* 74 (1959), 203-12.
W. H. Irving. *John Gay: Favorite of the Wits*. Durham, N. Carolina, 1940.
A. Sherbo. 'Virgil, Dryden, Gay, and Matters Trivial'. *Publications of the Modern Language Association of America* 85 (1970), 1063-71.
P. M. Spacks. *John Gay*. New York, 1965.
J. Sutherland. 'John Gay'. In *Pope and his Contemporaries: Essays Presented to George Sherburn*. Ed. J. L. Clifford and L. A. Landa. Oxford, 1949.
H. Trowbridge. 'Pope, Gay and *The Shepherd's Week*'. *Modern Language Quarterly* 5 (1944), 79-88.

WINE
[1708]
lines 1-67, 146-76, 193-222, 262-78.

Of Happiness Terrestrial, and the Source
Whence human pleasures flow, sing Heavenly Muse,
Of sparkling juices, of th'enliv'ning Grape,
Whose quickning tast adds vigour to the Soul,
5   Whose sov'raign pow'r revives decaying nature,
And thaws the frozen Blood of hoary Age
A kindly warmth diffusing, Youthful fires
Gild his dim Eyes, and paint with ruddy hue
His wrizzled Visage, ghastly wan before:
10   Cordial restorative, to mortal Man
With copious Hand by bounteous Gods bestow'd.

    BACCHUS Divine, aid my adventrous Song,
That with no middle flight intends to soar
Inspir'd, Sublime on Pegasean Wing
15   By thee upborn, I draw Miltonic Air.

    When fumy Vapours clog our loaded Brows
With furrow'd Frowns, when stupid downcast Eyes
Th'external Symptoms of remorse within,
Our Grief express, or when in sullen Dumps
20   With Head Incumbent on Expanded Palm,
Moaping we sit in silent sorrow drown'd:
Whether Inviegling Hymen has trappand
Th'unwary Youth, and ty'd the Gordian Knot
Of jangling Wedlock, Indissoluble;
25   Worried all Day by loud Xantippes Din,
And when the gentle Dew of sleep inclines
With slumbrous weight his Eye-lids, She inflam'd
With Uncloy'd Lust, and itch Insatiable,
His Stock exhausted, still yells on for more;
30   Nor fails She to Exalt him to the Stars,
And fix him there among the Branched Crew

(Taurus, and Aries, and Capricorn,)
The greatest Monster of the Zodiac;
Or for the loss of Anxious Worldly Pelf,
35 Or Celia's scornful slights, and cold disdain
Had check'd his Am'rous flame with coy repulse,
The worst Events that Mortals can befall;
By cares depress'd, in pensive Hypoish Mood,
With slowest pace, the tedious Minuits Roll.

40   Thy charming sight, but much more charming Gust
New Life incites, and warms our chilly Blood,
Strait with pert Looks, we raise our drooping fronts,
And pour in Chrystal pure, thy purer juice,
With chearful Countenance, and steady Hand
45 Raise it Lip-high, then fix the spatious Rim
T'expecting Mouth, and now with Grateful tast,
The ebbing Wine glides swiftly o're the Tongue,
The circling Blood with quicker motion flies;
Such is thy pow'rful influence, thou strait
50 Dispell'st those Clouds that lowring dark eclips'd
The whilom Glories of our gladsom Face,
And dimpled Cheeks, and sparkling rolling Eyes,
Thy chearing Virtues, and thy worth proclaim.
So Mists and Exhalations that arise
55 From Hills or steamy Lake, Dusky or Gray
Prevail, till Phæbus sheds Titanian Rays,
And paints their Fleecy skirts with shining Gold;
Unable to resist, the Foggy damps
That veild the surface of the verdant Fields,
60 At the Gods penetrating Beams disperse:
The Earth again in former Beauty smiles,
In gaudiest Livery drest, all Gay and Clear.

    When disappointed Strephon meets Repulse,
Scofft at, despis'd, in Melancholic mood
65 Joyless he wasts in sighs the lazy Hours,

Till Reinforc't by thy Almighty aid,
He Storms the Breach, and Wins the Beauteous Fort.
. . .

    But we, not as our Pristin sires, repair
T'umbrageous Grot or Vale, but when the Sun
Faintly from Western Skies his rays oblique
Darts sloping, and to Thetis watry Lap
150   Hastens in Prone Career, with Friends Select
Swiftly we hie to Devil Young or Old
Jocund and Boon, where at the entrance stands
A Stripling, who with Scrapes and Humil Cringe,
Greets us in winning Speech and Accent Bland;
155   With lightest bound, and safe unerring step
He skips before, and nimbly climbs the Stairs:
Melampus thus, panting with lolling Tongue,
And wagging Tail, Gamboles, and frisks before
His sequel Lord from pensive walk return'd,
160   Whether in Shady Wood, or Pastures Green,
And waits his coming at the well known Gate.
Nigh to the Stairs Ascent, in regal Port
Sits a Majestic Dame, whose looks denounce
Command and Sov'reignty, with haughty Air,
165   And Studied Mien, in Semicirc'lar Throne
Enclos'd, she deals around her dread Commands;
Behind her (Dazling sight) in order Rang'd,
Pile above Pile Chrystallin Vessels shine;
Attendant Slaves with eager stride advance,
170   And after Homage paid, bawl out aloud
Words Unintelligible, noise confus'd:
She knows the Jargon Sound, and strait describes
In Characters Mysterious Words obscure;
More legible are Algebraic Signs,
175   Or Mystic Figures by Magicians drawn,
When they Invoke aid Diabolical.
. . .

The Stairs Ascent now gain'd, our Guide unbars
The Door of Spatious Room, and creaking Chairs
195 (To ear offensive) round the Table sets,
We sit, when thus his Florid Speech begins:
Name, Sirs, the WINE that most invites your Tast,
Champaign or Burgundy, or Florence pure,
Or Hock Antique, or Lisbon New or Old,
200 Bourdeaux, or neat French White, or Alicant:
For Bourdeaux we with Voice Unanimous
Declare, (such Sympathy's in Boon Compeers.)
He quits the Room Alert, but soon returns,
One Hand Capacious glist'ring Vessels bore
205 Resplendant, th'other with a grasp secure,
A Bottle (mighty charge) upstaid, full Fraught
With goodly Wine, He with extended Hand
Rais'd high, pours forth the Sanguin frothy Juice,
O'respread with Bubbles, dissipated soon:
210 We strait t'our Arms repair, experienc't Chiefs;
Now Glasses clash with Glasses, (charming sound,)
And Glorious ANNA's Health the first the best
Crowns the full Glass, at HER inspiring Name
The sprightly Wine Results, and seems to Smile,
215 With hearty Zeal, and wish Unanimous
The Health we Drink, and in HER Health our own.

A Pause ensues, and now with grateful Chat
W' improve the Interval, and Joyous Mirth
Engages our rais'd Souls, Pat Repartee,
220 Or Witty Joke our airy Senses moves
To pleasant Laughter, strait the Ecchoing Room
With Universal Peals and Shouts Resounds.
. . .

Thus we the winged Hours in harmless Mirth,
And Joys Unsully'd pass, till Humid Night
Has half her Race perform'd, now all Abroad
265 Is hush'd and silent, nor the Rumbling noise

Of Coach or Cart, or smoaky Link-Boys call
Is heard; but Universal silence Reigns:
When we in Merry Plight, Airy and Gay,
Surpriz'd to find the Hours so swiftly flie,
270 With hasty knock, or Twang of Pendant Cord
Alarm the drowsy Youth from slumb'ring Nod;
Startled he flies, and stumbles o're the Stairs
Erroneous, and with busie Knuckles plies
His yet clung Eye-lids, and with stagg'ring Reel
275 Enters Confus'd, and Mutt'ring asks our Wills;
When we with Lib'ral Hand the Score discharge,
And Homeward each his Course with steady step
Unerring steer'd, of Cares and Coin bereft.

THE SHEPHERD'S WEEK
In Six Pastorals
[1714]

THE PROEME
To the Courteous READER

*Great Marvell hath it been, (and that not unworthily) to diverse worthy
Wits that in this our Island of Britain, in all rare Sciences so greatly
abounding, more especially in all kinds of Poesie highly flourishing,
no Poet (though otherways of notable Cunning in Roundelays) hath
hit on the right simple Eclogue after the true ancient guise of Theo-
critus, before this mine Attempt.*

*Other Poet travailing in this plain High-way of Pastoral know I
none. Yet, certes, such it behoveth a Pastoral to be, as Nature in the
Country affordeth; and the Manners also meetly copied from the
rustical Folk therein. In this also my Love to my native Country
Britain much pricketh me forward, to describe aright the Manners of
our own honest and laborious Plough-men, in no wise sure more un-
worthy a British Poet's imitation, than those of Sicily or Arcadie; al-
beit, not ignorant I am, what a Rout and Rabblement of Critical
Gallimawfry hath been made of late Days by certain young Men of*

insipid Delicacy, concerning, I wist not what, Golden Age, and other outragious Conceits, to which they would confine Pastoral. Whereof, I avow, I account nought at all, knowing no Age so justly to be instiled Golden, as this of our Soveraign Lady Queen ANNE.

This idle Trumpery (only fit for Schools and Schoolboys) unto that ancient Dorick Shepherd Theocritus, or his Mates, was never known; he rightly, throughout his fifth Idyll, maketh his Louts give foul Language, and behold their Goats at Rut in all Simplicity.

> [The goatherd, seeing the nanny-goats covered,
>   weeps that he is not a goat.
>
> Theocritus, *Idylls* 1. 87-88]

Verily, as little Pleasance receiveth a true homebred Tast, from all the fine finical new-fangled Fooleries of this gay Gothic Garniture, wherewith they so nicely bedeck their Court Clowns, or Clown Courtiers, (for, which to call them rightly, I wot not) as would a prudent Citizen journeying to his Country Farms, should he find them occupied by People of this motley Make, instead of plain down-right hearty cleanly Folk; such as be now Tenants to the wealthy Burgesses of this Realme.

Furthermore, it is my Purpose, gentle Reader, to set before thee, as it were a Picture, or rather lively Landscape of thy own Country, just as thou mightest see it, didest thou take a Walk into the Fields at the proper Season: even as Maister Milton hath elegantly set forth the same.

> As one who long in populous City pent,
> Where Houses thick and Sewers annoy the Aire,
> Forth issuing on a Summer's Morn to breathe
> Among the pleasant Villages and Farms
> Adjoin'd, from each thing met conceives Delight;
> The Smell of Grain or tedded Grass or Kine
> Or Dairie, each rural Sight, each rural Sound.
>
> [*Paradise Lost*, 9. 445-51]

Thou wilt not find my Shepherdesses idly piping on oaten Reeds, but milking the Kine, tying up the Sheaves, or if the Hogs are astray driving them to their Styes. My Shepherd gathereth none other Nose-gays but what are the growth of our own Fields, he sleepeth not under Myrtle shades, but under a Hedge, nor doth he vigilantly

defend his Flocks from Wolves, because there are none, as Maister
Spencer well observeth.

> Well is known that since the Saxon King
> Never was Wolf seen, many or some
> Nor in all Kent nor in Christendom.

[*Shepheardes Calender*, 'September' 151-53]

For as much, as I have mentioned Maister Spencer, soothly I must
acknowledge him a Bard of sweetest Memorial. Yet hath his Shepherds
Boy at some times raised his rustick Reed to Rhimes more rumbling
than rural. Diverse grave Points also hath he handled of Churchly
Matter and Doubts in Religion daily arising, to great Clerkes only
appertaining. What liketh me best are his Names, indeed right simple
and meet for the Country, such as Lobbin, Cuddy, Hobbinol, Diggon,
and others, some of which I have made bold to borrow. Moreover, as
he called his Eclogues, the Shepherd's Calendar, *and divided the same*
into the twelve Months, I have chosen (paradventure not overrashly)
to name mine by the Days of the Week, omitting Sunday or the
Sabbath, Ours being supposed to be Christian Shepherds, and to be
then at Church Worship. Yet further of many of Maister Spencer's
Eclogues it may be observed; though Months they be called, of the
said Months therein, nothing is specified; wherein I have also esteemed
him worthy mine Imitation.

That principally, courteous Reader, whereof I would have thee to
be advertised, (seeing I depart from the vulgar Usage) is touching the
Language of my Shepherds; which is, soothly to say, such as is neither
spoken by the country Maiden nor the courtly Dame; nay, not only
such as in the present Times is not uttered, but was never uttered in
Times past; and, if I judge aright, will never be uttered in Times future.
It having too much of the Country to be fit for the Court; too much
of the Court to be fit for the Country, too much of the Language
of old Times to be fit for the Present, too much of the Present
to have been fit for the Old, and too much of both to be fit for
any time to come. Granted also it is, that in this my Language,
I seem unto myself, as a London Mason, who calculateth his Work
for a Term of Years, when he buildeth with old Materials upon
a Ground-rent that is not his own, which soon turneth to Rub-
bish and Ruins. For this point, no Reason can I alledge, only deep

learned Ensamples having led me thereunto.

But here again, much Comfort ariseth in me, from the Hopes, in that I conceive, when these Words in the course of transitory Things shall decay, it may so hap, in meet time that some Lover of Simplicity shall arise, who shall have the Hardiness to render these mine Eclogues into such more modern Dialect as shall be then understood, to which end, Glosses and Explications of uncouth Pastoral Terms are annexed.

Gentle Reader, turn over the Leaf, and entertain thyself with the Prospect of thine own Country, limned by the painful Hand of

thy Loving Countryman
JOHN GAY.

MONDAY; OR, THE SQUABBLE
Lobbin Clout, Cuddy, Cloddipole

Lobbin Clout
Thy Younglings, Cuddy, are but just awake,
No Thrustles shrill the Bramble-Bush forsake,
No chirping Lark the Welkin sheen invokes,
No Damsel yet the swelling Udder strokes;
5   O'er yonder Hill does scant the Dawn appear,
Then why does Cuddy leave his Cott, so rear?

Cuddy
    Ah Lobbin Clout! I ween, my Plight is guest,
For *he that loves, a Stranger is to Rest*;
If Swains belye not, thou hast prov'd the Smart,
10   And Blouzelinda's Mistress of thy Heart.

3. Welkin *the same as* Welken, *an old* Saxon *Word signifying* a Cloud *by Poetical Licence it is frequently taken for* the Element *or* Sky, *as may appear by this Verse in the Dream of* Chaucer. Ne in all the Welkin was no Cloud. Sheen *or* Shine, *an old Word for* shining *or* bright.
5. Scant, *used in ancient* British *Authors for* scarce.
6. Rear, *an Expression in several Counties of* England, *for* early in the Morning.
7. To ween, *derived from the* Saxon, *to* think *or* conceive.

This rising rear betokeneth well thy Mind,
Those Arms are folded for thy Blouzelind.
And well, I trow, our piteous Plights agree,
Thee Blouzelinda smites, Buxoma me.

Lobbin Clout
15   Ah Blouzelind! I love thee more by half,
Than Does their Fawns, or Cows the new-fall'n Calf:
Woe worth the Tongue! may Blisters sore it gall,
That names Buxoma, Blouzelind withal.

Cuddy
    Hold, witless Lobbin Clout, I thee advise,
20   Lest Blisters sore on thy own Tongue arise.
Lo yonder Cloddipole, the blithesome Swain,
The wisest Lout of all the neighbouring Plain.
From Cloddipole we learnt to read the Skies,
To know when Hail will fall, or Winds arise.
25   He taught us erst the Heifers Tails to view,
When stuck aloft, that Show'rs would strait ensue;
He first that useful Secret did explain,
That pricking Corns foretold the gath'ring Rain.
When Swallows fleet soar high and sport in Air,
30   He told us that the Welkin wou'd be clear.
Let Cloddipole then hear us twain rehearse,
And praise his Sweetheart in alternate Verse.
I'll wager this same Oaken Staff with thee,
That Cloddipole shall give the Prize to me.

Lobbin Clout
35   See this Tobacco Pouch that's lin'd with Hair,
Made of the Skin of sleekest fallow Deer.
This Pouch, that's ty'd with Tape of reddest Hue,
I'll wager, that the Prize shall be my due.

---

25. Erst, *a Contraction of* ere this, *it signifies* sometime ago *or* formerly.

Cuddy

    Begin thy Carrols then, thou vaunting Slouch,
40   Be thine the Oaken Staff, or mine the Pouch.

Lobbin Clout

    My Blouzelinda is the blithest Lass,
Than Primrose sweeter, or the Clover-Grass.
Fair is the King-Cup that in Meadow blows,
Fair is the Daisie that beside her grows,
45   Fair is the Gillyflow'r, of Gardens sweet,
Fair is the Mary-Gold, for Pottage meet.
But Blouzelind's than Gillyflow'r more fair,
Than Daisie, Mary-Gold, or King-Cup rare.

Cuddy

    My brown Buxoma is the featest Maid,
50   That e'er at Wake delightsome Gambol play'd.
Clean as young Lambkins or the Goose's Down,
And like the Goldfinch in her Sunday Gown.
The witless Lambs may sport upon the Plain,
The frisking Kid delight the gaping Swain,
55   The wanton Calf may skip with many a Bound,
And my Cur Tray play deftest Feats around:
But neither Lamb nor Kid, nor Calf nor Tray,
Dance like Buxoma on the first of May.

Lobbin Clout

    Sweet is my Toil when Blouzelind is near,
60   Of her bereft 'tis Winter all the Year.
With her no sultry Summer's Heat I know;
In Winter, when she's nigh, with Love I glow.
Come Blouzelinda, ease thy Swain's Desire,
My Summer's Shadow and my Winter's Fire!

56. Deft, *an old Word signifying* brisk *or* nimble.

Cuddy

65   As with Buxoma once I work'd at Hay,
Ev'n Noon-tide Labour seem'd an Holiday;
And Holidays, if haply she were gone,
Like Worky-days I wish'd would soon be done.
Eftsoons, O Sweet-heart kind, my Love repay,
70   And all the Year shall then be Holiday.

Lobbin Clout

    As Blouzelinda in a gamesome Mood,
Behind a Haycock loudly laughing stood,
I slily ran, and snatch'd a hasty Kiss,
She wip'd her Lips, nor took it much amiss.
75   Believe me, Cuddy, while I'm bold to say,
Her Breath was sweeter than the ripen'd Hay.

Cuddy

    As my Buxoma in a Morning fair,
With gentle Finger stroak'd her milky Care,
I queintly stole a Kiss; at first, 'tis true
80   She frown'd, yet after granted one or two.
Lobbin, I swear, believe who will my Vows,
Her Breath by far excell'd the breathing Cows.

Lobbin Clout

    Leek to the Welch, to Dutchmen Butter's dear,
Of Irish Swains Potatoe is the Chear;

69. Ettsoons, *from* eft *an ancient* British *Word signifying* soon. *So that* eftsoons *is a doubling of the Word* soon, *which is, as it were to say* twice soon, *or very soon.*

79. Queint *has various Significations in the ancient* English *Authors. I have used it in this Place in the same Sense as* Chaucer *hath done in his* Miller's Tale. *As* Clerkes been full subtil and queint, *(by which he means* Arch *or* Waggish) *and not in that obscene Sense wherein he useth it in the Line immediately following.*

83. *Populus Alcidæ gratissima, vitis Iaccho,*
Fermosæ Myrtus Veneri, sua Laurea Phœbo.
Phillis amat Corylos. Illas dum Phillis amabit,
Nec Myrtus vincet Corylos nec Laurea Phœbi. &c.   Virg.

85   Oats for their Feasts the Scottish Shepherds grind,
     Sweet Turnips are the Food of Blouzelind.
     While she loves Turnips, Butter I'll despise.
     Nor Leeks nor Oatmeal nor Potatoe prize.

Cuddy
      In good Roast Beef my Landlord sticks his Knife,
90 The Capon fat delights his dainty Wife,
     Pudding our Parson eats, the Squire loves Hare,
     But White-pot thick is my Buxoma's Fare.
     While she loves White-pot, Capon ne'er shall be,
     Nor Hare, nor Beef, nor Pudding, Food for me.

Lobbin Clout
95   As once I play'd at Blindman's-buff, it hapt
     About my Eyes the Towel thick was wrapt.
     I miss'd the Swains, and seiz'd on Blouzelind;
     True speaks that ancient Proverb, *Love is blind*.

Cuddy
      As at Hot-Cockles once I laid me down,
100 And felt the weighty Hand of many a Clown;
     Buxoma gave a gentle Tap, and I
     Quick rose, and read soft Mischief in her Eye.

Lobbin Clout
      On two near Elms, the slacken'd Cord I hung,
     Now high, now low my Blouzelinda swung.
105 With the rude Wind her rumpled Garment rose,
     And show'd her taper Leg, and scarlet Hose.

Cuddy
      Across the fallen Oak the Plank I laid,
     And my self pois'd against the tott'ring Maid,
     High leapt the Plank; adown Buxoma fell;
110 I spy'd—but faithful Sweethearts never tell.

Lobbin Clout
    This Riddle, Cuddy, if thou canst, explain,
This wily Riddle puzzles ev'ry Swain.
† *What Flower is that which bears the* Virgin's *Name,*
The richest Metal joined with the same?

Cuddy
115   Answer, thou Carle, and judge this Riddle right,
I'll frankly own thee for a cunning Wight.
* *What Flow'r is that which Royal Honour craves,*
Adjoin the Virgin, *and 'tis strown on Graves.*

Cloddipole
    Forbear, contending Louts, give o'er your Strains,
120 An Oaken Staff each merits for his Pains.
But see the Sun-Beams bright to Labour warn,
And gild the Thatch of Goodman Hodges' Barn.
Your Herds for want of Water stand adry,
They're weary of your Songs—and so am I.

WEDNESDAY; OR, THE DUMPS

Sparabella
    The Wailings of a Maiden I recite,
A Maiden fair, that Sparabella hight.
Such Strains ne'er warble in the Linnets Throat,
Nor the gay Goldfinch chaunts so sweet a Note,
5   No Mag-pye chatter'd, nor the painted Jay,
Nor Ox was heard to low, nor Ass to bray.
No rusling Breezes play'd the Leaves among,
While thus her Madrigal the Damsel sung.

---

117. *Dic quibus in terris inscripti nomina Regum*
     Nascantur Flores. Virg. †*Marygold.* **Rosemary.*
120. *Et vitula tu dignus & hic.* Virg.

A while, O D ['Urfe] y, lend an Ear or twain,
10   Nor, though in homely Guise, my verse disdain;
Whether thou seek'st new Kingdoms in the Sun,
Whether thy Muse does at New-Market run,
Or does with Gossips at a Feast regale,
And heighten her Conceits with Sack and Ale,
15   Or else at Wakes with Joan and Hodge rejoice,
Where D ['Urfe] y's Lyricks swell in every Voice;
Yet suffer me, thou Bard of wond'rous Meed,
Amid thy Bays to weave this rural Weed.

Now the Sun drove adown the western Road,
20   And Oxen laid at rest forget the Goad,
The Clown fatigu'd trudg'd homeward with his Spade,
Across the Meadows stretch'd the lengthen'd Shade;
When Sparabella pensive and forlorn,
Alike with yearning Love and Labour worn,
25   Lean'd on her Rake, and strait with doleful Guise
Did this sad Plaint in moanful Notes devise.

Come Night as dark as Pitch, surround my Head,
From Sparabella Bumkinet is fled;
The Ribbon that his val'rous Cudgel won,
30   Last Sunday happier Clumsilis put on.
Sure, if he'd Eyes (*but Love, they say, has none*)
I whilome by that Ribbon had been known.
Ah, Well-a-day! I'm shent with baneful Smart,
For with the Ribbon he bestow'd his Heart.
35   *My plaint, ye Lasses, with this Burthen aid,*
'Tis hard so true a Damsel dies a Maid.

Shall heavy Clumsilis with me compare?
View this, ye Lovers, and like me despair.
Her blubber'd Lip by smutty Pipes is worn,
40   And in her breath Tobacco Whiffs are born;
The cleanly Cheese-press she could never turn,
Her awkward Fist did ne'er employ the Churn;

If e'er she brew'd, the Drink would strait grow sour,
Before it ever felt the Thunder's Pow'r:
45   No Huswifry the dowdy Creature knew;
To sum up all, her Tongue confess'd the Shrew.
    My Plaint, ye Lasses, with this Burthen aid,
    'Tis hard so true a Damsel dies a Maid.

    I've often seen my Visage in yon Lake,
50   Nor are my Features of the homeliest Make.
Though Clumsilis may boast a whiter Dye,
Yet the black Sloe turns in my rolling Eye;
And fairest Blossoms drop with ev'ry Blast,
But the brown Beauty will like Hollies last.
55   Her wan Complexion's like the wither'd Leek,
While Katherine Pears adorn my ruddy Cheek.
Yet she, alas! the witless Lout hath won,
And by her Gain, poor Sparabell's undone!
Let Hares and Hounds in coupling Straps unite,
60   The clocking Hen make Friendship with the Kite,
Let the Fox simply wear the Nuptial Noose,
And join in Wedlock with the wadling Goose;
For Love hath brought a stranger thing to pass,
The fairest Shepherd weds the foulest Lass.
65   *My Plaint, ye Lasses, with this Burthen aid,*
    'Tis hard so true a Damsel dies a Maid.

    Sooner shall Cats disport in Waters clear,
And speckled Mackrel graze the Meadows fair,
Sooner shall scriech Owls bask in Sunny Day,
70   And the slow Ass on Trees, like Squirrels, play,
Sooner shall Snails on insect Pinions rove,
Than I forget my Shepherd's wonted Love!
    My Plaint, ye Lasses, with this Burthen aid,
    'Tis hard so true a Damsel dies a Maid.

75   Ah! didst thou know what Proffers I withstood
When late I met the Squire in yonder Wood!

To me he sped, regardless of his Game,
Whilst all my Cheek was glowing red with Shame;
My lip he kiss'd, and prais'd my healthful Look,
80   Then from his Purse of Silk a Guinea took,
Into my Hand he forc'd the tempting Gold,
While I with modest struggling broke his Hold.
He swore that Dick in Liv'ry strip'd with Lace,
Should wed me soon to keep me from Disgrace;
85   But I nor Footman priz'd nor golden Fee,
For what is Lace or Gold compar'd to thee?
    My Plaint, ye Lasses, with this Burthen aid,
'Tis hard so true a Damsel dies a Maid.

Now plain I ken whence Love his Rise begun.
90   Sure he was born some bloody Butcher's Son,
Bred up in Shambles, where our Younglings slain,
Erst taught him Mischief and to sport with Pain.
The Father only silly Sheep annoys,
The Son, the sillier Shepherdess destroys.
95   Does Son or Father greater Mischief do?
The Sire is cruel, so the Son is too.
    My Plaint, ye Lasses, with this Burthen aid,
'Tis hard so true a Damsel dies a Maid.

Farewel, ye Woods, ye Meads, ye Streams that flow;
100   A sudden Death shall rid me of my Woe.
This Penknife keen my Windpipe shall divide.—
What, shall I fall as squeaking Pigs have dy'd!
No—To some Tree this Carcass I'll suspend.—
But worrying Curs find such untimely End!
105   I'll speed me to the Pond, where the high Stool
On the long Plank hangs o'er the muddy Pool,
That Stool, the dread of ev'ry scolding Quean.—
Yet, sure a Lover should not dye so mean!
There plac'd aloft, I'll rave and rail by Fits,
110   Though all the Parish say I've lost my Wits;
And thence, if Courage holds, my self I'll throw,

And quench my Passion in the Lake below.
Ye Lasses, cease your Burthen, cease to moan,
And, by my Case forewarn'd, go mind your own.

115   The Sun was set; the Night came on a-pace,
And falling Dews bewet around the Place,
The Bat takes airy Rounds on leathern Wings,
And the hoarse Owl his woeful Dirges sings;
The prudent Maiden deems it now too late,
120 And 'till to Morrow comes, defers her Fate.

SATURDAY; OR, THE FLIGHTS

Bowzybeus
    Sublimer Strains, O rustick Muse, prepare;
Forget a-while the Barn and Dairy's Care;
Thy homely Voice to loftier Numbers raise,
The Drunkard's Flights require sonorous Lays,
5   With Bowzybeus' Songs exalt thy Verse,
While Rocks and Woods the various Notes rehearse.

    'Twas in the Season when the Reaper's Toil
Of the ripe Harvest 'gan to rid the Soil;
Wide through the Field was seen a goodly Rout,
10 Clean Damsels bound the gather'd Sheaves about,
The Lads with sharpen'd Hook and sweating Brow
Cut down the Labours of the Winter Plow.
To the near Hedge young Susan steps aside,
She feign'd her Coat or Garter was unty'd,
15 What-e'er she did, she stoop'd adown unseen,
And merry Reapers, what they list, will ween.
Soon she rose up, and cry'd with Voice so shrill
That Eccho answer'd from the distant Hill;
The Youths and Damsels ran to Susan's Aid,
20 Who thought some Adder had the Lass dismay'd.

When fast asleep they Bowzybeus spy'd,
His Hat and oaken Staff lay close beside:
That Bowzybeus who could sweetly sing,
Or with the rozin'd Bow torment the String;
25   That Bowzybeus who with Finger's speed
Could call soft Warblings from the breathing Reed;
That Bowzybeus who with jocund Tongue,
Ballads and Roundelays and Catches sung.
They loudly laugh to see the Damsel's Fright,
30   And in disport surround the drunken Wight.

Ah Bowzybee, why didst thou stay so long,
The Mugs were large, the Drink was wondrous strong!
Thou should'st have left the Fair before 'twas Night,
But thou sat'st toping 'till the Morning Light.

35   Cic'ly, brisk Maid, steps forth before the Rout,
And kiss'd with smacking Lip the snoring Lout.
For Custom says, *Who-e'er this Venture Proves,*
For such a Kiss demands a pair of Gloves.
By her Example Dorcas bolder grows,
40   And plays a tickling Straw within his Nose.
He rubs his Nostril, and in wonted Joke
The sneering Swains with stamm'ring Speech bespoke.
To you, my Lads, I'll sing my Carrols o'er,
As for the Maids,—I've something else in store.

45   No sooner 'gan he raise his tuneful Song,
But Lads and Lasses round about him throng.
Not Ballad-singer plac'd above the Croud
Sings with a Note so shrilling sweet and loud,
Nor Parish Clerk who calls the Psalm so clear,
50   Like Bowzybeus sooths th' attentive Ear.

Of Nature's Laws his Carrols first begun,
Why the grave Owl can never face the Sun.
For Owles, as Swains observe, detest the Light,

And only sing and seek their Prey by Night.
55 How Turnips hide their swelling Heads below,
    And how the closing Colworts upwards grow;
    How Will-a-Wisp mis-leads Night-faring Clowns,
    O'er Hills, and sinking Bogs, and pathless Downs.
    Of Stars he told that shoot with shining Trail,
60 And of the Glow-worms Light that gilds his Tail.
    He sung where Wood-cocks in the Summer feed,
    And in what Climates they renew their Breed;
    Some think to Northern Coasts their Flight they tend,
    Or to the Moon in Midnight Hours ascend.
65 Where Swallows in the Winter's Season keep,
    And how the drowsie Bat and Dormouse sleep.
    How Nature does the Puppy's Eyelid close,
    'Till the bright Sun has nine times set and rose.
    For Huntsmen by their long Experience find,
70 That Puppys still nine rolling Suns are blind.

    Now he goes on, and sings of Fairs and Shows,
    For still new Fairs before his Eyes arose.
    How Pedlars Stalls with glitt'ring Toys are laid,
    The various Fairings of the Country Maid.
75 Long silken Laces hang upon the Twine,
    And Rows of Pins and amber Bracelets shine;
    How the tight Lass, Knives, Combs and Scissars spys,
    And looks on Thimbles with desiring Eyes.
    Of Lott'ries next with tuneful Note he told,
80 Where silver Spoons are won and Rings of Gold.
    The Lads and Lasses trudge the Street along,
    And all the Fair is crouded in his Song.
    The Mountebank now treads the Stage, and sells
    His Pills, his Balsoms, and his Ague spells;
85 Now o'er and o'er the nimble Tumbler springs,
    And on the Rope the vent'rous Maiden swings;
    Jack-pudding in his parti-coloured Jacket
    Tosses the Glove and jokes at ev'ry Packet.

Of Raree-Shows he sung, and Punch's Feats,
90   Of Pockets pick'd in Crowds, and various Cheats.

Then sad he sung *the Children in the Wood.*
Ah barb'rous Uncle, stain'd with Infant Blood!
How Blackberrys they pluck'd in Desarts wild,
And fearless at the glittering Fauchion smil'd;
95   Their little Corps the Robin-red-breasts found,
And strow'd with pious Bill the Leaves around.
Ah gentle Birds! if this Verse lasts so long,
Your Names shall live for ever in my Song.

For Buxom Joan he sung the doubtful Strife,
100 How the sly Sailor made the Maid a Wife.

To louder Strains he rais'd his Voice, to tell
What woeful Wars in *Chevy-Chace* befell,
When *Piercy drove the Deer with Hound and Horn,*
Wars to be wept by Children yet unborn!
105 Ah With'rington, more Years thy Life had crown'd,
If thou had'st never heard the Horn or Hound!
Yet shall the Squire, who fought on bloody Stumps,
By future Bards be wail'd in doleful Dumps.

All in the Land of Essex next he chaunts,
110 How to sleek Mares starch Quakers turn Gallants;
How the grave Brother stood on Bank so green.
Happy for him if Mares had never been!

Then he was seiz'd with a religious Qualm,
And on a sudden, sung the hundredth Psalm.

115   He sung of *Taffey-Welch*, and *Sawney Scot*,
Lilly-bullero and the *Irish Trot.*
Why should I tell of *Bateman* or of *Shore*,
Or *Wantley's Dragon* slain by valiant *Moore*,

The Bow'r of Rosamond, or *Robin Hood*,
120   And how the *Grass now grows where* Troy Town *stood?*

       His Carrols ceas'd: The list'ning Maids and Swains
       Seem still to hear some soft imperfect Strains.
       Sudden he rose; and as he reels along
       Swears Kisses sweet should well reward his Song.
125   The Damsels laughing fly: the giddy Clown
       Again upon a Wheat-Sheaf drops adown;
       The Pow'r that Guards the Drunk, his Sleep attends,
       'Till, ruddy, like his Face, the Sun descends.

TRIVIA
Or, the Art of Walking the Streets of London
[1716]

BOOK I
Of the Implements for walking the Streets, and Signs of
the Weather

       Through Winter Streets to steer your Course aright,
       How to walk clean by Day, and safe by Night,
       How jostling Crouds, with Prudence, to decline,
       When to assert the Wall, and when resign,
5   I sing: Thou Trivia, Goddess, aid my Song,
       Thro' spacious Streets conduct thy Bard along:
       By thee transported, I securely stray
       Where winding Alleys lead the doubtful Way,
       The silent Court, and op'ning Square explore,
10   And long perplexing Lanes untrod before.
       To pave thy Realm, and smooth the broken Ways,
       Earth from her Womb a flinty Tribute pays;
       For thee, the sturdy Pavior thumps the Ground,
       Whilst ev'ry Stroke his lab'ring Lungs resound;

15   For thee, the Scavinger bids Kennels glide
      Within their Bounds, and Heaps of Dirt subside.
      My youthful Bosom burns with Thirst of Fame,
      From the great Theme to build a glorious Name,
      To tread in Paths to ancient Bards unknown,
20   And bind my Temples with a Civic Crown;
      But more, my Country's Love demands the Lays,
      My Country's be the Profit, mine the Praise.

Of Shoes
         When the Black Youth at chosen Stands rejoice,
      And *clean your Shoes* resounds from ev'ry Voice;
25   When late their miry Sides Stage-Coaches show,
      And their stiff Horses thro' the Town move slow;
      When all the Mall in leafy Ruin lies,
      And Damsels first renew their Oyster Cries:
      Then let the prudent Walker Shoes provide,
30   Not of the Spanish or Morocco Hide;
      The wooden Heel may raise the Dancer's Bound,
      And with the 'scallop'd Top his Step be crown'd:
      Let firm, well-hammer'd Soles protect thy Feet
      Thro' freezing Snows, and Rains, and soaking Sleet.
35   Should the big Laste extend the Shoe too wide,
      Each Stone will wrench th'unwary Step aside:
      The sudden Turn may stretch the swelling Vein,
      Thy cracking Joint unhinge, or Ankle sprain;
      And when too short the modish Shoes are worn,
40   You'll judge the Seasons by your shooting Corn.

Of Coats
         Nor should it prove thy less important Care,
      To chuse a proper coat for Winter's Wear.
      Now in thy Trunk thy Doily Habit fold,
      The silken Drugget ill can fence the Cold;
45   The Frieze's spongy Nap is soak'd with Rain,
      And Show'rs soon drench the Camlet's cockled Grain.
      True Witney Broad-cloath with it's Shag unshorn,

Unpierc'd is in the lasting Tempest worn:
Be this the Horse-man's Fence; for who would wear
50   Amid the Town the Spoils of Russia's Bear?
Within the Roquelaure's Clasp thy Hands are pent,
Hands, that stretch'd forth invading Harms prevent.
Let the loop'd Bavaroy the Fop embrace,
Or his deep Cloak be spatter'd o'er with Lace.
55   That Garment best the Winter's Rage defends,
Whose shapeless Form in ample Plaits depends;
By †various Names in various Counties known,
Yet held in all the true Surtout alone:
Be thine of Kersey firm, though small the Cost,
60   Then brave unwet the Rain, unchill'd the Frost.

Of Canes

     If the strong Cane support thy walking Hand,
Chairmen no longer shall the Wall command;
Ev'n sturdy Car-men shall thy Nod obey,
And rattling Coaches stop to make thee Way:
65   This shall direct thy cautious Tread aright,
Though not one glaring Lamp enliven Night.
Let Beaus their Canes with Amber tipt produce,
Be theirs for empty Show, but thine for Use.
In gilded Chariots while they loll at Ease,
70   And lazily insure a Life's Disease;
While softer Chairs the tawdry Load convey
To Court, to *White's, Assemblies, or the Play;
Rosie-complexion'd Health thy Steps attends,
And Exercise thy lasting Youth defends.
75   Imprudent Men Heav'ns choicest Gifts prophane.
Thus some beneath their Arm support the Cane;
The dirty Point oft checks the careless Pace,
And miry Spots thy clean Cravat disgrace:
O! may I never such Misfortune meet,

† A Joseph, a Wrap-Rascal, &c. [Gay]
 * White's Chocolate-House in St. James's Street. [Gay]

80   May no such vicious Walkers croud the Street,
     May Providence o'er-shade me with her Wings,
     While the bold Muse experienc'd Dangers sings.

       Not that I wander from my native Home,
     And tempting Perils foreign Cities roam.
85   Let Paris be the Theme of Gallia's Muse,
     Where Slav'ry treads the Streets in wooden Shoes;
     Nor do I rove in Belgia's frozen Clime,
     And teach the clumsy Boor to skate in Rhyme,
     Where, if the warmer Clouds in Rain descend,
90   No miry Ways industrious Steps offend,
     The rushing Flood from sloping Pavements pours,
     And blackens the Canals with dirty Show'rs.
     Let others Naples smoother Streets rehearse,
     And with proud Roman Structures grace their Verse,
95   Where frequent Murders wake the Night with Groans,
     And Blood in purple Torrents dies the Stones;
     Nor shall the Muse through narrow Venice stray,
     Where Gondolas their painted Oars display.
     O happy Streets to rumbling Wheels unknown,
100   No Carts, no Coaches shake the floating Town!
     Thus was of old Britannia's City bless'd,
     E'er Pride and Luxury her Sons possess'd:
     Coaches and Chariots yet unfashion'd lay,
     Nor late invented Chairs perplex'd the Way:
105   Then the proud Lady trip'd along the Town,
     And tuck'd up Petticoats secur'd her Gown,
     Her rosie Cheek with distant Visits glow'd,
     And Exercise unartful Charms bestow'd;
     But since in braided Gold her Foot is bound,
110   And a long trailing Manteau sweeps the Ground,
     Her Shoe disdains the Street; the lazy Fair,
     With narrow Step affects a limping Air.
     Now gaudy Pride corrupts the lavish Age,
     And the Streets flame with glaring Equipage;
115   The tricking Gamester insolently rides,

With Loves and Graces on his Chariot's Sides;
In sawcy State the griping Broker sits,
And laughs at Honesty, and trudging Wits:
For you, O honest Men, these useful Lays
120 The Muse prepares; I seek no other Praise.

Of the Weather
When Sleep is first disturb'd by Morning Cries;
From sure Prognosticks learn to know the Skies,
Lest you of Rheums and Coughs at Night complain;
Surpriz'd in dreary Fogs, or driving Rain.
125 When suffocating Mists obscure the Morn,
Let thy worst Wig, long us'd to Storms, be worn;
This knows the powder'd Footman, and with Care,
Beneath his flapping Hat, secures his Hair.
Be thou, for ev'ry Season, justly drest,
130 Nor brave the piercing Frost with open Breast;
And when the bursting Clouds a Deluge pour,
Let thy Surtout defend the drenching Show'r.

Signs of cold Weather
The changing Weather certain Signs reveal.
E'er Winter sheds her Snow, or Frosts congeal,
135 You'll see the Coals in brighter Flame aspire,
And Sulphur tinge with blue the rising Fire:
Your tender Shins the scorching Heat decline,
And at the Dearth of Coals the Poor repine;
Before her Kitchin Hearth, the nodding Dame
140 In Flannel Mantle wrapt, enjoys the Flame;
Hov'ring, upon her feeble Knees she bends,
And all around the grateful Warmth ascends.

Signs of fair Weather
Nor do less certain Signs the Town advise,
Of milder Weather, and serener Skies.
145 The Ladies gayly dress'd, the Mall adorn
With various Dyes, and paint the sunny Morn;

The wanton Fawns with frisking Pleasure range,
And chirping Sparrows greet the welcome Change:
Not that their Minds with greater Skill are fraught,
150 Endu'd by Instinct, or by Reason taught,
The Seasons operate on every Breast;
'Tis hence that Fawns are brisk, and Ladies drest.
When on his Box the nodding Coachman snores,
And dreams of fancy'd Fares; when Tavern Doors
155 The Chairmen idly croud; then ne'er refuse
To trust thy busy Steps in thinner Shoes.

Signs of rainy Weather
    But when the swinging Signs your Ears offend
With creaking Noise, then rainy Floods impend;
Soon shall the Kennels swell with rapid Streams,
160 And rush in muddy Torrents to the Thames.
The Bookseller, whose Shop's an open Square,
Foresees the Tempest, and with early Care
Of Learning strips the Rails; the rowing Crew
To tempt a Fare, cloath all their Tilts in Blue:
165 On Hosier's Poles depending Stockings ty'd,
Flag with the slacken'd Gale, from side to side;
Church-Monuments foretell the changing Air;
Then Niobe dissolves into a Tear,
And sweats with secret Grief; you'll hear the Sounds
170 Of whistling Winds, e'er Kennels break their Bounds;
Ungrateful Odours Common-shores diffuse,
And dropping Vaults distil unwholesom Dews,
E'er the Tiles rattle with the smoaking Show'r,
And Spouts on heedless Men their Torrents pour.

Superstition to be avoided
175   All Superstition from thy Breast repel.
Let cred'lous Boys, and prattling Nurses tell,
How, if the Festival of Paul be clear,
Plenty from lib'ral Horn shall strow the Year;
When the dark Skies dissolve in Snows or Rain,

180   The lab'ring Hind shall yoke the Steer in vain;
But if the threatning Winds in Tempests roar,
Then War shall bathe her wasteful Sword in Gore.
How, if on Swithin's Feast the Welkin lours,
And ev'ry Penthouse streams with hasty Show'rs,
185   Twice twenty Days shall Clouds their Fleeces drain,
And wash the Pavements with incessant Rain.
Let not such vulgar Tales debase thy Mind;
Nor Paul nor Swithin rule the Clouds and Wind.

If you the Precepts of the Muse despise,
190   And slight the faithful Warnings of the Skies,
Others you'll see, when all the Town's afloat,
Wrapt in th'Embraces of a Kersey Coat,
Or double-button'd Freize; their guarded Feet
Defie the muddy Dangers of the Street,
195   While you, with Hat unloop'd, the Fury dread
Of Spouts high-streaming, and with cautious Tread
Shun ev'ry dashing Pool; or idly stop,
To seek the kind Protection of a Shop.
But Bus'ness summons; Now with hasty Scud
200   You jostle for the Wall; the spatter'd Mud
Hides all thy Hose behind; in vain you scow'r,
Thy Wig alas! uncurl'd, admits the Show'r.
So fierce Alecto's snaky Tresses fell,
When Orpheus charm'd the rig'rous Pow'rs of Hell.
205   Or thus hung Glaucus' Beard, with briny Dew
Clotted and strait, when first his am'rous View
Surpris'd the bathing Fair; the frighted Maid
Now stands a Rock, transform'd by Circe's Aid.

Implements proper for female Walkers
Good Huswives all the Winter's Rage despise,
210   Defended by the Riding-hood's Disguise;
Or underneath th' Umbrella's oily Shed,
Safe thro' the Wet on clinking Pattens tread.
Let Persian Dames th' Umbrella's Ribs display,

To guard their Beauties from the sunny Ray;
215   Or sweating Slaves support the shady Load,
When Eastern Monarchs shew their State abroad;
Britain in Winter only knows its Aid,
To guard from chilly Show'rs the walking Maid.
But, O! forget not, Muse, the Patten's Praise,
220   That female Implement shall grace thy Lays;
Say from what Art Divine th' Invention came,
And from its Origine deduce the Name.

An Episode of the Invention of Pattens
Where Lincoln wide extends her fenny Soil,
A goodly Yeoman liv'd grown white with Toil;
225   One only Daughter blest his nuptial Bed,
Who from her infant Hand the Poultry fed:
Martha (her careful Mother's Name) she bore,
But now her careful Mother was no more.
Whilst on her Father's Knee the Damsel play'd,
230   Patty he fondly call'd the smiling Maid;
As Years increas'd, her ruddy Beauty grew,
And Patty's Fame o'er all the Village flew.

Soon as the blushing Morning warms the Skies,
And in the doubtful Day the Woodcock flies,
235   Her cleanly Pail the pretty Huswife bears,
And singing to the distant Field repairs:
And when the Plains with ev'ning Dews are spread,
The milky Burthen smoaks upon her Head.
Deep, thro' a miry Lane she pick'd her Way,
240   Above her Ankle rose the chalky Clay.

Vulcan, by chance the bloomy Maiden spies,
With Innocence and Beauty in her Eyes,
He saw, he lov'd; for yet he ne'er had known
Sweet Innocence and Beauty meet in One.
245   Ah Mulciber! recall thy nuptial Vows,
Think on the Graces of thy Paphian Spouse,

Think how her Eyes dart inexhausted Charms,
And canst thou leave her Bed for Patty's Arms?

  The Lemnian Pow'r forsakes the Realms above,
250 His Bosom glowing with terrestrial Love:
Far in the Lane, a lonely Hut he found,
No Tenant ventur'd on th' unwholesome Ground.
Here smoaks his Forge, he bares his sinewy Arm,
And early Strokes the sounding Anvil warm;
255 Around his Shop the steely Sparkles flew,
As for the Steed he shap'd the bending Shoe.

  When blue-eye'd Patty near his Window came,
His Anvil rests, his Forge forgets to flame.
To hear his soothing Tales, she feigns Delays;
260 What Woman can resist the Force of Praise?

  At first she coyly ev'ry Kiss withstood,
And all her Cheek was flush'd with modest Blood:
With headless Nails he now surrounds her Shoes,
To save her Steps from Rains and piercing Dews;
265 She lik'd his soothing Tales, his Presents wore,
And granted Kisses, but would grant no more.
Yet Winter chill'd her Feet, with Cold she pines,
And on her Cheek the fading Rose declines;
No more her humid Eyes their Lustre boast,
270 And in hoarse Sounds her melting Voice is lost.

  This Vulcan saw, and in his heav'nly Thought,
A new Machine Mechanick Fancy wrought,
Above the Mire her shelter'd Steps to raise,
And bear her safely through the Wintry Ways.
275 Strait the new Engine on his Anvil glows,
And the pale Virgin on the Patten rose.
No more her Lungs are shook with dropping Rheums,
And on her Cheek reviving Beauty blooms.
The God obtain'd his Suit, though Flatt'ry fail,

280   Presents with Female Virtue must prevail.
       The Patten now supports each frugal Dame,
       Which from the blue-ey'd Patty takes the Name.

BOOK III
Of Walking the Streets by Night

     O Trivia, Goddess, leave these low Abodes,
     And traverse o'er the wide Ethereal Roads,
     Celestial Queen, put on thy Robes of Light,
     Now Cynthia nam'd, fair Regent of the Night.
5   At Sight of thee, the Villain sheaths his Sword,
     Nor scales the Wall, to steal the wealthy Hoard.
     Oh! may thy Silver Lamp in Heav'n's high Bow'r
     Direct my Footsteps in the Midnight Hour.

The Evening
     When Night first bids the twinkling Stars appear,
10   Or with her cloudy Vest inwraps the Air,
     Then swarms the busie Street; with Caution tread,
     Where the Shop-Windows falling threat thy Head;
     Now Lab'rers home return, and join their Strength
     To bear the tott'ring Plank, or Ladder's Length;
15   Still fix thy Eyes intent upon the Throng,
     And as the Passes open, wind along.

Of the Pass of St. Clements
     Where the fair Columns of Saint Clement stand,
     Whose straiten'd Bounds encroach upon the Strand;
     Where the low Penthouse bows the Walker's Head,
20   And the rough Pavement wounds the yielding Tread;
     Where not a Post protects the narrow Space,
     And strung in Twines, Combs dangle in thy Face;
     Summon at once thy Courage, rouze thy Care,
     Stand firm, look back, be resolute, beware.
25   Forth issuing from steep Lanes, the Collier's Steeds

Drag the black Load; another Cart succeeds,
Team follows Team, Crouds heap'd on Crouds appear,
And wait impatient, 'till the Road grow clear.
Now all the Pavement sounds with trampling Feet,
30   And the mixt Hurry barricades the Street.
Entangled here, the Waggon's lengthen'd Team
Crack the tough Harness; Here a pond'rous Beam
Lies over-turn'd athwart; For Slaughter fed,
Here lowing Bullocks raise their horned Head.
35   Now Oaths grow loud, with Coaches Coaches jar,
And the smart Blow provokes the sturdy War;
From the high Box they whirl the Thong around,
And with the twining Lash their Shins resound:
Their Rage ferments, more dang'rous Wounds they try,
40   And the Blood gushes down their painful Eye.
And now on Foot the frowning Warriors light,
And with their pond'rous Fists renew the Fight;
Blow answers Blow, their Cheeks are 'smear'd with Blood,
'Till down they fall, and grappling roll in Mud.
45   So when two Boars, in wild *Ytene bred,
Or on Westphalia's fatt'ning Chest-nuts fed,
Gnash their sharp Tusks, and rous'd with equal Fire,
Dispute the Reign of some luxurious Mire;
In the black Flood they wallow o'er and o'er,
50   'Till their arm'd Jaws distill with Foam and Gore.

Of Pick-Pockets
    Where the Mob gathers, swiftly shoot along,
Nor idly mingle in the noisy Throng.
Lur'd by the Silver Hilt, amid the Swarm,
The subtil Artist will thy Side disarm.
55   Nor is thy Flaxen Wigg with Safety worn;
High on the Shoulder, in the Basket born,
Lurks the sly Boy; whose Hand to Rapine bred,
Plucks off the curling Honours of the Head.

* New Forest in Hampshire, anciently so called. [Gay]

Here dives the skulking Thief, with practis'd Slight,
60   And unfelt Fingers make thy Pocket light.
Where's now thy Watch, with all its Trinkets, flown?
And thy late Snuff-Box is no more thy own.
But lo! his bolder Thefts some Tradesman spies,
Swift from his Prey the scudding Lurcher flies;
65   Dext'rous he scapes the Coach, with nimble Bounds,
While ev'ry honest Tongue *Stop Thief* resounds.
So speeds the wily Fox, alarm'd by Fear,
Who lately filch'd the Turkey's callow Care;
Hounds following Hounds, grow louder as he flies,
70   And injur'd Tenants joyn the Hunter's Cries.
Breathless he stumbling falls: Ill-fated Boy!
Why did not honest Work thy Youth employ?
Seiz'd by rough Hands, he's dragg'd amid the Rout,
And stretch'd beneath the Pump's incessant Spout:
75   Or plung'd in miry Ponds, he gasping lies,
Mud choaks his Mouth, and plaisters o'er his Eyes.

Of Ballad-Singers
Let not the Ballad-Singer's shrilling Strain
Amid the Swarm thy list'ning Ear detain:
Guard well thy Pocket; for these Syrens stand,
80   To aid the Labours of the diving Hand;
Confed'rate in the Cheat, they draw the Throng,
And Cambrick Handkerchiefs reward the Song.
But soon as Coach or Cart drives rattling on,
The Rabble part, in Shoals they backward run.
So Jove's loud Bolts the mingled War divide,
And Greece and Troy retreats on either side.

Of walking with a Friend
If the rude Throng pour on with furious Pace,
And hap to break thee from a Friend's Embrace,
Stop short; nor struggle thro' the Croud in vain,
90   But watch with careful Eye the passing Train.
Yet I (perhaps too fond) if chance the Tide

Tumultuous, bears my Partner from my Side,
Impatient venture back; despising Harm,
I force my Passage where the thickest swarm.
95 Thus his lost Bride the Trojan sought in vain
Through Night, and Arms, and Flames, and Hills of Slain.
Thus Nisus wander'd o'er the pathless Grove,
To find the brave Companion of his Love,
The pathless Grove in vain he wanders o'er:
100 Euryalus alas! is now no more.

Of inadvertent Walkers
That Walker, who regardless of his Pace,
Turns oft' to pore upon the Damsel's Face,
From Side to Side by thrusting Elbows tost,
Shall strike his aking Breast against the Post;
105 Or Water, dash'd from fishy Stalls, shall stain
His hapless Coat with Spirts of scaly Rain.
But if unwarily he chance to stray,
Where twirling Turnstiles intercept the Way,
The thwarting Passenger shall force them round,
110 And beat the Wretch half breathless to the Ground.

Useful Precepts
Let constant Vigilance thy Footsteps guide,
And wary Circumspection guard thy Side;
Then shalt thou walk unharm'd the dang'rous Night,
Nor need th'officious Link-Boy's smoaky Light.
115 Thou never wilt attempt to cross the Road,
Where Alehouse Benches rest the Porter's Load,
Grievous to heedless Shins; No Barrow's Wheel,
That bruises oft' the Truant School-Boy's Heel,
Behind thee rolling, with insidious Pace,
120 Shall mark thy Stocking with a miry Trace.
Let not thy vent'rous Steps approach too nigh,
Where gaping wide, low steepy Cellars lie;
Should thy Shoe wrench aside, down, down you fall,
And overturn the scolding Huckster's Stall,

125   The scolding Huckster shall not o'er thee moan,
        But Pence exact for Nuts and Pears o'erthrown.

Safety first of all to be consider'd
        Though you through cleanlier Allies wind by Day,
        To shun the Hurries of the publick Way,
        Yet ne'er to those dark Paths by Night retire;
130   Mind only Safety, and contemn the Mire.
        Then no impervious Courts thy Haste detain,
        Nor sneering Ale-Wives bid thee turn again.

The Danger of crossing a Square by Night
        Where Lincoln's-Inn, wide Space, is rail'd around,
        Cross not with vent'rous Step; there oft' is found
135   The lurking Thief, who while the Day-light shone,
        Made the Walls eccho with his begging Tone:
        That Crutch which late Compassion mov'd, shall wound
        Thy bleeding Head, and fell thee to the Ground.
        Though thou art tempted by the Link-man's Call,
140   Yet trust him not along the lonely Wall;
        In the Mid-way he'll quench the flaming Brand,
        And share the Booty with the pilf'ring Band.
        Still keep the publick Streets, where oily Rays
        Shot from the Crystal Lamp, o'erspread the Ways.

The Happiness of London
145   Happy Augusta! Law-defended Town!
        Here no dark Lanthorns shade the Villain's Frown;
        No Spanish Jealousies thy Lanes infest,
        Nor Roman Vengeance stabs th' unwary Breast;
        Here Tyranny ne'er lifts her purple Hand,
150   But Liberty and Justice guard the Land;
        No Bravos here profess the bloody Trade,
        Nor is the Church the Murd'rer's Refuge made.

Of Chairmen
>   Let not the Chairman, with assuming Stride,
>   Press near the Wall, and rudely thrust thy Side:
> 155 The Laws have set him Bounds; his servile Feet
>   Should ne'er encroach where Posts defend the Street.
>   Yet who the Footman's Arrogance can quell,
>   Whose Flambeau gilds the Sashes of Pell-Mell?
>   When in long Rank a Train of Torches flame,
> 160 To light the Midnight Visits of the Dame?
>   Others, perhaps, by happier Guidance led,
>   May where the Chairman rests, with Safety tread;
>   Whene'er I pass, their Poles unseen below,
>   Make my Knee tremble with the jarring Blow.

Of crossing the Street
> 165   If Wheels bar up the Road, where Streets are crost,
>   With gentle Words, the Coachman's Ear accost:
>   He ne'er the Threat, or harsh Command obeys,
>   But with Contempt the spatter'd Shoe surveys.
>   Now man with utmost Fortitude thy Soul,
> 170 To cross the Way where Carts and Coaches roll;
>   Yet do not in thy hardy Skill confide,
>   Nor rashly risque the Kennel's spacious Stride;
>   Stay till afar the distant Wheel you hear,
>   Like dying Thunder in the breaking Air;
> 175 Thy Foot will slide upon the miry Stone,
>   And passing Coaches crush thy tortur'd Bone,
>   Or Wheels enclose the Road; on either Hand
>   Pent round with Perils, in the midst you stand,
>   And call for Aid in vain; the Coachman swears,
> 180 And Carmen drive, unmindful of thy Prayers.
>   Where wilt thou turn? ah! whither wilt thou fly?
>   On ev'ry side the pressing Spokes are nigh.
>   So Sailors, while Charybdis' Gulphs they shun,
>   Amaz'd, on Scylla's craggy Dangers run.

Of Oysters

185   Be sure observe where brown Ostrea stands,
        Who boasts her shelly Ware from Wallfleet Sands;
        There may'st thou pass, with safe unmiry Feet,
        Where the rais'd Pavement leads athwart the Street.
        If where Fleet-Ditch with muddy Current flows,
190   You chance to roam; where Oyster-Tubs in Rows
        Are rang'd beside the Posts; there stay thy Haste,
        And with the sav'ry Fish indulge thy Taste:
        The Damsel's Knife the gaping Shell commands,
        While the salt Liquor streams between her Hands.

195   The Man had sure a Palate cover'd o'er
        With Brass or Steel, that on the rocky Shore
        First broke the oozy Oyster's pearly Coat,
        And risqu'd the living Morsel down his Throat.
        What will not Lux'ry taste? Earth, Sea, and Air
200   Are daily ransack'd for the Bill of Fare.
        Blood stuff'd in Skins is British Christian's Food,
        And France robs Marshes of the croaking Brood;
        Spungy Morells in strong Ragousts are found,
        And in the Soupe the slimy Snail is drown'd.

Observations concerning keeping the Wall

205   When from high Spouts the dashing Torrents fall,
        Ever be watchful to maintain the Wall;
        For should'st thou quit thy Ground, the rushing Throng
        Will with impetuous Fury drive along;
        All press to gain those Honours thou hast lost,
210   And rudely shove thee far without the Post.
        Then to retrieve the Shed you strive in vain,
        Draggled all o'er, and soak'd in Floods of Rain.
        Yet rather bear the Show'r, and Toils of Mud,
        Than in the doubtful Quarrel risque thy Blood.
215   O think on Œdipus' detested State,
        And by his Woes be warn'd to shun thy Fate.

Where three Roads join'd, he met his Sire unknown;
(Unhappy Sire, but more unhappy Son!)
Each claim'd the Way, their Swords the Strife decide,
220 The hoary Monarch fell, he groan'd and dy'd!
Hence sprung the fatal Plague that thinn'd thy Reign,
Thy cursed Incest! and thy Children slain!
Hence wert thou doom'd in endless Night to stray
Through Theban Streets, and cheerless groap thy Way.

Of a Funeral

225·   Contemplate, Mortal, on thy fleeting Years;
See, with black Train the Funeral Pomp appears!
Whether some Heir attends in sable State,
And mourns with outward Grief a Parent's Fate;
Or the fair Virgin, nipt in Beauty's Bloom,
230 A Croud of Lovers follow to her Tomb.
Why is the Herse with 'Scutcheons blazon'd round,
And with the nodding Plume of Ostrich crown'd?
No: The Dead know it not, nor Profit gain;
It only serves to prove the Living vain.
235 How short is Life! how frail is human Trust!
Is all this Pomp for laying Dust to Dust?

Of avoiding Paint

Where the nail'd Hoop defends the painted Stall,
Brush not thy sweeping Skirt too near the Wall;
Thy heedless Sleeve will drink the colour'd Oil,
240 And Spot indelible thy Pocket soil.
Has not wise Nature strung the Legs and Feet
With firmest Nerves, design'd to walk the Street?
Has she not given us Hands, to groap aright,
Amidst the frequent Dangers of the Night?
245 And think'st thou not the double Nostril meant,
To warn from oily Woes by previous Scent?

Of various Cheats formerly in practice

     Who can the various City Frauds recite,
     With all the petty Rapines of the Night?
     Who now the Guinea-Dropper's Bait regards,
250 Trick'd by the Sharper's Dice, or Juggler's Cards?
     Why shou'd I warn thee ne'er to join the Fray,
     Where the Sham-Quarrel interrupts the Way?
     Lives there in these our Days so soft a Clown,
     Brav'd by the Bully's Oaths, or threat'ning Frown?
255 I need not strict enjoyn the Pocket's Care,
     When from the crouded Play thou lead'st the Fair;
     Who has not here, or Watch, or Snuff-Box lost,
     Or Handkerchiefs that India's Shuttle boast?

An Admonition to Virtue

     O! may thy Virtue guard thee through the Roads
260 Of Drury's mazy Courts, and dark Abodes,
     The Harlots' guileful Paths, who nightly stand,
     Where Katherine-street descends into the Strand.
     Say, vagrant Muse, their Wiles and subtil Arts,
     To lure the Stranger's unsuspecting Hearts;
265 So shall our Youth on healthful Sinews tread,
     And City Cheeks grow warm with rural Red.

How to know a Whore

     'Tis She who nightly strowls with saunt'ring Pace,
     No stubborn Stays her yielding Shape embrace;
     Beneath the Lamp her tawdry Ribbons glare,
270 The new-scower'd Manteau, and the slattern Air;
     High-draggled Petticoats her Travels show,
     And hollow Cheeks with artful Blushes glow;
     With flatt'ring Sounds she sooths the cred'lous Ear,
     My noble Captain! Charmer! Love! my Dear!
275 In Riding-hood, near Tavern-Doors she plies,
     Or muffled Pinners hide her livid Eyes.
     With empty Bandbox she delights to range,
     And feigns a distant Errand from the Change;

Nay, she will oft' the Quaker's Hood prophane,
280 And trudge demure the Rounds of Drury-Lane.
She darts from Sarsnet Ambush wily Leers,
Twitches thy Sleeve, or with familiar Airs,
Her Fan will pat thy Cheek; these Snares disdain,
Nor gaze behind thee, when she turns again.

A dreadful Example
285   I knew a Yeoman, who for thirst of Gain,
To the great City drove from Devon's Plain
His num'rous lowing Herd; his Herds he sold,
And his deep leathern Pocket bagg'd with Gold;
Drawn by a fraudful Nymph, he gaz'd, he sigh'd;
290 Unmindful of his Home, and distant Bride,
She leads the willing Victim to his Doom,
Through winding Alleys to her Cobweb Room.
Thence thro' the Street he reels, from Post to Post,
Valiant with Wine, nor knows his Treasure lost.
295 The vagrant Wretch th' assembled Watchmen spies,
He waves his Hanger, and their Poles defies;
Deep in the Round-House pent, all Night he snores,
And the next Morn in vain his Fate deplores.

    Ah hapless Swain, unus'd to Pains and Ills!
300 Canst thou forgo Roast-Beef for nauseous Pills?
How wilt thou lift to Heav'n thy Eyes and Hands,
When the long Scroll the Surgeon's Fees demands!
Or else (ye Gods avert that worst Disgrace)
Thy ruin'd Nose falls level with thy Face,
305 Then shall thy Wife thy loathsome Kiss disdain,
And wholesome Neighbours from thy Mug refrain.

Of Watchmen
    Yet there are Watchmen, who with friendly Light,
Will teach thy reeling Steps to tread aright;
For Sixpence will support thy helpless Arm,
310 And Home conduct thee, safe from nightly Harm;

But if they shake their Lanthorns, from afar,
To call their Breth'ren to confed'rate War,
When Rakes resist their Pow'r; if hapless you
Should chance to wander with the scow'ring Crew;
315 Though Fortune yield thee Captive, ne'er despair,
But seek the Constable's consid'rate Ear;
He will reverse the Watchman's harsh Decree,
Mov'd by the Rhet'rick of a Silver Fee.
Thus would you gain some fav'rite Courtier's Word;
320 Fee not the petty Clarks, but bribe my Lord.

Of Rakes

Now is the Time that Rakes their Revells keep;
Kindlers of Riot, Enemies of Sleep.
His scatter'd Pence the flying *Nicker flings,
And with the Copper Show'r the Casement rings.
325 Who has not heard the Scowrer's Midnight Fame?
Who has not trembled at the Mohock's Name?
Was there a Watchman took his hourly Rounds,
Safe from their Blows, or new-invented Wounds?
I pass their desp'rate Deeds, and Mischiefs done,
330 Where from Snow-hill black steepy Torrents run;
How Matrons, hoop'd within the Hogshead's Womb,
Were tumbled furious thence, the rolling Tomb
O'er the Stones thunders, bounds from Side to Side.
So Regulus to save his Country dy'd.

A necessary Caution in a dark Night

335 Where a dim Gleam the paly Lanthorn throws
O'er the mid' Pavement; heapy Rubbish grows,
Or arched Vaults their gaping Jaws extend,
Or the dark Caves to Common-Shores descend.
Oft' by the Winds, extinct the Signal lies,
340 Or smother'd in the glimm'ring Socket dies,
E'er Night has half roll'd round her Ebon Throne;

* Gentlemen, who delighted to break Windows with Half-pence. [Gay]

In the wide Gulph the shatter'd Coach o'erthrown,
Sinks with the snorting Steeds; the Reins are broke,
And from the cracking Axle flies the Spoke.
345 So when fam'd Eddystone's far-shooting Ray,
That led the Sailor through the stormy Way,
Was from its rocky Roots by Billows torn,
And the high Turret in the Whirlewind born,
Fleets bulg'd their Sides against the craggy Land,
350 And pitchy Ruines blacken'd all the Strand.

Who then through Night would hire the harness'd Steed,
And who would chuse the rattling Wheel for Speed?

A Fire
But hark! Distress with screaming Voice draws nigh'r,
And wakes the slumb'ring Street with Cries of Fire.
355 At first a glowing Red enwraps the Skies,
And born by Winds the scatt'ring Sparks arise;
From Beam to Beam, the fierce Contagion spreads;
The spiry Flames now lift aloft their Heads,
Through the burst Sash a blazing Deluge pours,
360 And splitting Tiles descend in rattling Show'rs.
Now with thick Crouds th'enlighten'd Pavement swarms,
The Fire-man sweats beneath his crooked Arms,
A leathern Casque his vent'rous Head defends,
Boldly he climbs where thickest Smoak ascends;
365 Mov'd by the Mother's streaming Eyes and Pray'rs,
The helpless Infant through the Flame he bears,
With no less Virtue, than through hostile Fire,
The Dardan Hero bore his aged Sire.
See forceful Engines spout their levell'd Streams,
370 To quench the Blaze that runs along the Beams;
The grappling Hook plucks Rafters from the Walls,
And Heaps on Heaps the smoaky Ruine falls.
Blown by strong Winds the fiery Tempest roars,
Bears down new Walls, and pours along the Floors:
375 The Heav'ns are all a-blaze, the Face of Night

Is cover'd with a sanguine dreadful Light;
'Twas such a Light involv'd thy Tow'rs, O Rome,
The dire Presage of mighty Cæsar's Doom,
When the Sun veil'd in Rust his mourning Head,
380   And frightful Prodigies the Skies o'erspread.
Hark! the Drum thunders! far, ye Crouds, retire:
Behold! the ready Match is tipt with Fire,
The nitrous Store is laid, the smutty Train
With running Blaze awakes the barrell'd Grain;
385   Flames sudden wrap the Walls; with sullen Sound,
The shatter'd Pile sinks on the smoaky Ground.
So when the Years shall have revolv'd the Date,
Th' inevitable Hour of Naples' Fate,
Her sap'd Foundations shall with Thunders shake,
390   And heave and toss upon the sulph'rous Lake;
Earth's Womb at once the fiery Flood shall rend,
And in th' Abyss her plunging Tow'rs descend.

      Consider, Reader, what Fatigues I've known,
The Toils, the Perils of the wintry Town;
395   What Riots seen, what bustling Croud I bor'd,
How oft' I cross'd where Carts and Coaches roar'd;
Yet shall I bless my Labours, if Mankind
Their future Safety from my Dangers find.
Thus the bold Traveller, inur'd to Toil,
400   Whose Steps have printed Asia's desert Soil,
The Barb'rous Arabs Haunt; or shiv'ring crost
Dark Greenland Mountains of eternal Frost;
Whom Providence, in length of Years, restores
To the wish'd Harbour of his native Shores;
405   Sets forth his Journals to the publick View,
To caution, by his Woes, the wandring Crew.

      And now compleat my gen'rous Labours lye,
Finish'd, and ripe for Immortality.
Death shall entomb in Dust this mould'ring Frame
410   But never reach th'eternal Part, my Fame.

When W[ard] and G[ildon], mighty Names, are dead;
Or but at Chelsea under Custards read;
When Criticks crazy Bandboxes repair,
And Tragedies, turn'd Rockets, bounce in Air;
415 High-rais'd on Fleetstreet Posts, consign'd to Fame,
This Work shall shine, and Walkers bless my name.

ECLOGUES
[*Poems on Several Occasions*, 1720]

THE BIRTH of the SQUIRE
An ECLOGUE
In Imitation of the POLLIO of VIRGIL

Ye sylvan Muses, loftier strains recite,
Not all in shades, and humble cotts delight.
Hark! the bells ring; along the distant ground
The driving gales convey the swelling sounds;
5 Th' attentive swain, forgetful of his work,
With gaping wonder, leans upon his fork.
What sudden news alarms the waking morn?
To the glad Squire a hopeful heir is born.
Mourn, mourn, ye stags; and all ye beasts of chase,
10 This hour destruction brings on all your race:
See the pleas'd tenants duteous off'rings bear,
Turkeys and geese and grocer's sweetest ware;
With the new health the pond'rous tankard flows,
And old October reddens ev'ry nose.
15 Beagles and spaniels round his cradle stand,
Kiss his moist lip and gently lick his hand;
He joys to hear the shrill horn's ecchoing sounds,
And learns to lisp the names of all the hounds.
With frothy ale to make his cup o'er-flow,
20 Barley shall in paternal acres grow;

The bee shall sip the fragrant dew from flow'rs,
To give metheglin for his morning hours;
For him the clustring hop shall climb the poles,
And his own orchard sparkle in his bowles.
25   His Sire's exploits he now with wonder hears,
The monstrous tales indulge his greedy ears;
How when youth strung his nerves and warm'd his veins
He rode the mighty Nimrod of the plains:
He leads the staring infant through the hall,
30   Points out the horny spoils that grace the wall;
Tells, how this stag thro' three whole Countys fled,
What rivers swam, where bay'd, and where he bled.
Now he the wonders of the fox repeats,
Describes the desp'rate chase, and all his cheats;
35   How in one day beneath his furious speed,
He tir'd sev'n coursers of the fleetest breed;
How high the pale he leapt, how wide the ditch,
When the hound tore the haunches of the *witch!
These storys which descend from son to son,
40   The forward boy shall one day make his own.
      Ah, too fond mother, think the time draws nigh,
That calls the darling from thy tender eye;
How shall his spirit brook the rigid rules,
And the long tyranny of grammar schools?
45   Let younger brothers o'er dull authors plod,
Lash'd into Latin by the tingling rod;
No, let him never feel that smart disgrace:
Why should he wiser prove than all his race?
      When rip'ning youth with down o'ershades his chin,
50   And ev'ry female eye incites to sin;
The milk-maid (thoughtless of her future shame)
With smacking lip shall raise his guilty flame;
The dairy, barn, the hay-loft and the grove
Shall oft' be conscious of their stolen love.

* The most common accident to Sportsmen;
  to hunt a witch in the shape of a hare. [Gay]

55 But think, Priscilla, on that dreadful time,
　　When pangs and watry qualms shall own thy crime;
　　How wilt thou tremble when thy Nipple's prest,
　　To see the white drops bathe thy swelling breast!
　　Nine moons shall publickly divulge thy shame,
60 And the young Squire forestall a father's name.
　　　　When twice twelve times the reaper's sweeping hand
　　With levell'd harvests has bestrown the land,
　　On fam'd St. Hubert's feast, his winding horn
　　Shall cheer the joyful hound and wake the morn:
65 This memorable day his eager speed
　　Shall urge with bloody heel the rising steed.
　　O check the foamy bit, nor tempt thy fate,
　　Think on the murders of a five-bar gate!
　　Yet prodigal of life, the leap he tries,
70 Low in the dust his groveling honour lies,
　　Headlong he falls, and on the rugged stone
　　Distorts his neck, and cracks the collar bone;
　　O vent'rous youth, thy thirst of game allay,
　　Mayst thou survive the perils of this day!
75 He shall survive; and in late years be sent
　　To snore away Debates in Parliament.
　　　　The time shall come, when his more solid sense
　　With nod important shall the laws dispense;
　　A Justice with grave Justices shall sit,
80 He praise their wisdom, they admire his wit.
　　No greyhound shall attend the tenant's pace,
　　No rusty gun the farmer's chimney grace;
　　Salmons shall leave their covers void of fear,
　　Nor dread the thievish net or triple spear;
85 Poachers shall tremble at his awful name,
　　Whom vengeance now o'ertakes for murder'd game.
　　　　Assist me, Bacchus, and ye drunken Pow'rs,
　　To sing his friendships and his midnight hours!
　　　　Why dost thou glory in thy strength of beer,
90 Firm-cork'd, and mellow'd till the twentieth year;
　　Brew'd or when Phœbus warms the fleecy sign,

Or when his languid rays in Scorpio shine.
Think on the mischiefs which from hence have sprung!
It arms with curses dire the wrathful tongue;
95 Foul scandal to the lying lip affords,
And prompts the mem'ry with injurious words.
O where is wisdom, when by this o'erpower'd?
The State is censur'd, and the maid deflower'd!
And wilt thou still, O Squire, brew ale so strong?
100 Hear then the dictates of prophetic song.
Methinks I see him in his hall appear,
Where the long table floats in clammy beer,
'Midst mugs and glasses shatter'd o'er the floor,
Dead-drunk his servile crew supinely snore;
105 Triumphant, o'er the prostrate brutes he stands,
The mighty bumper trembles in his hands;
Boldly he drinks, and like his glorious Sires,
In copious gulps of potent ale expires.

THE TEA-TABLE
A Town ECLOGUE
Doris and Melanthe

Saint James's noon-day bell for prayers had toll'd,
And coaches to the Patron's Levée roll'd,
When Doris rose. And now through all the room
From flow'ry Tea exhales a fragrant fume.
5 Cup after cup they sipt, and talk'd by fits,
For Doris here and there Melanthe sits.
Doris was young, a laughter-loving dame,
Nice of her own alike and others fame;
Melanthe's tongue could well a tale advance,
10 And sooner gave than sunk a circumstance;
Lock'd in her mem'ry secrets never dy'd;
Doris begun, Melanthe thus reply'd.

Doris
Sylvia the vain fantastic Fop admires,
The Rake's loose gallantry her bosom fires;
15   Sylvia like that is vain, like this she roves,
In liking them she but her self approves.

Melanthe
Laura rails on at men, the sex reviles,
Their vice condemns, or at their folly smiles.
Why should her tongue in just resentment fail,
20   Since men at her with equal freedom rail?

Doris
Last Masquerade was Sylvia nymphlike seen,
Her hand a crook sustain'd, her dress was green;
An am'rous shepherd led her through the croud,
The nymph was innocent, the shepherd vow'd;
25   But nymphs their innocence with shepherds trust;
So both withdrew, as nymph and shepherd must.

Melanthe
Name but the licence of the modern stage,
Laura takes fire, and kindles into rage;
The whining Tragic love she scarce can bear,
30   But nauseous Comedy ne'er shock'd her ear;
Yet in the gall'ry mob'd, she sits secure,
And laughs at jests that turn the Box demure.

Doris
Trust not, ye Ladys, to your beauty's pow'r,
For beauty withers, like a shrivell'd flow'r;
35   Yet those fair flow'rs that Sylvia's temples bind,
Fade not with sudden blights or winter's wind;
Like those her face defys the rolling years,
For art her roses and her charms repairs.

Melanthe
Laura despises ev'ry outward grace,
40   The wanton sparkling eye, the blooming face;
The beauties of the soul are all her pride,
For other beauties Nature has deny'd;
If affectation show a beauteous mind,
Lives there a man to Laura's merits blind?

Doris
45   Sylvia be sure defies the town's reproach,
Whose Deshabille is soil'd in hackney coach;
What though the sash was clos'd? must we conclude,
That she was yielding, when her Fop was rude?

Melanthe
Laura learnt caution at too dear a cost.
50   What Fair could e'er retrieve her honour lost?
Secret she loves; and who the nymph can blame,
Who durst not own a footman's vulgar flame?

Doris
Though Laura's homely taste descends so low;
Her footman well may vye with Sylvia's Beau.

Melanthe
55   Yet why should Laura think it a disgrace,
When proud Miranda's groom wears Flander's lace?

Doris
What, though for musick Cynthio boasts an ear?
Robin perhaps can hum an Opera air.
Cynthio can bow, takes snuff, and dances well,
60   Robin talks common sense, can write and spell;
Sylvia's vain fancy dress and show admires,
But 'tis the man alone who Laura fires.

Melanthe
Plato's wise morals Laura's soul improve:
And this no doubt must be Platonic love!
65 Her soul to gen'rous acts was still inclin'd;
What shows more virtue than an humble mind?

Doris
What, though young Sylvia love the Park's cool shade,
And wander in the dusk the secret glade?
Masqu'd and alone (by chance) she met her Spark,
70 That innocence is weak which shuns the dark.

Melanthe
But Laura for her flame has no pretence;
Her footman is a footman too in sense.
All Prudes I hate, and those are rightly curst
With scandal's double load, who censure first.

Doris
75 And what if Cynthio Sylvia's garter ty'd!
Who such a foot and such a leg would hide;
When crook-knee'd Phillis can expose to view
Her gold-clock'd stocking, and her tawdry shoe?

Melanthe
If pure Devotion center in the face,
80 If cens'ring others show intrinsick grace,
If guilt to publick freedoms be confin'd,
Prudes (all must own) are of the holy kind!

Doris
Sylvia disdains reserve, and flys constraint:
She neither is, nor would be thought a Saint.

Melanthe
85 Love is a trivial passion, Laura crys,
May I be blest with friendship's stricter tyes;

To such a breast all secrets we commend;
Sure the whole Drawing-room is Laura's friend.

Doris
At marriage Sylvia rails; who men would trust?
90 Yet husband's jealousies are sometimes just.
Her favours Sylvia shares among mankind,
Such gen'rous love should never be confin'd.

      As thus alternate chat employ'd their tongue,
With thund'ring raps the brazen knocker rung.
95 Laura with Sylvia came; the nymphs arise:
This unexpected visit, Doris crys,
Is doubly kind! Melanthe Laura led,
Since I was last so blest, my dear, she said,
Sure 'tis an age! they sate; the hour was set;
100 And all again that night at Ombre met.

FABLES, 1727

INTRODUCTION TO THE FABLES
The Shepherd and the Philosopher

      Remote from citys liv'd a Swain,
Unvex'd with all the cares of gain,
His head was silver'd o'er with age,
And long experience made him sage;
5   In summer's heat and winter's cold
He fed his flock and pen'd the fold,
His hours in cheerful labour flew,
Nor envy nor ambition knew;
His wisdom and his honest fame
10   Through all the country rais'd his name.

A deep Philosopher (whose rules
Of moral life were drawn from schools)
The Shepherd's homely cottage sought,
And thus explor'd his reach of thought.
15   Whence is thy learning? Hath thy toil
O'er books consum'd the midnight oil?
Hast thou old Greece and Rome survey'd,
And the vast sense of Plato weigh'd?
Hath Socrates thy soul refin'd,
20   And hast thou fathom'd Tully's mind?
Or, like the wise Ulysses thrown
By various fates on realms unknown,
Hast thou through many citys stray'd,
Their customs, laws and manners weigh'd?
25   The Shepherd modestly reply'd.
I ne'er the paths of learning try'd,
Nor have I roam'd in foreign parts
To read mankind, their laws and arts;
For man is practis'd in disguise,
30   He cheats the most discerning eyes:
Who by that search shall wiser grow,
When we ourselves can never know?
The little knowledge, I have gain'd,
Was all from simple nature drain'd;
35   Hence my life's maxims took their rise,
Hence grew my settled hate to vice.
      The daily labours of the bee
Awake my soul to industry.
Who can observe the careful ant,
40   And not provide for future want?
My dog (the trustiest of his kind)
With gratitude inflames my mind;
I mark his true, his faithful way,
And in my service copy Tray.
45   In constancy, and nuptial love
I learn my duty from the dove.
The hen, who from the chilly air

With pious wing protects her care,
And ev'ry fowl that flies at large
50   Instructs me in a parent's charge.
      From nature too I take my rule
To shun contempt and ridicule.
I never with important air
In conversation overbear;
55   Can grave and formal pass for wise,
When men the solemn owl despise?
My tongue within my lips I rein,
For who talks much must talk in vain;
We from the wordy torrent fly:
60   Who listens to the chatt'ring pye?
Nor would I with felonious slight
By stealth invade my neighbour's right;
Rapacious animals we hate:
Kites, hawks and wolves deserve their fate.
65   Do not we just abhorrence find
Against the toad and serpent kind?
But envy, calumny and spite
Bear stronger venom in their bite.
Thus ev'ry object of creation
70   Can furnish hints to contemplation,
And from the most minute and mean
A virtuous mind can morals glean.
      Thy fame is just, the Sage replys,
Thy virtue proves thee truly wise;
75   Pride often guides the author's pen,
Books as affected are as men,
But he who studys nature's laws
From certain truth his maxims draws,
And those, without our schools, suffice
80   To make men moral, good and wise.

The Elephant and the Bookseller

    The man, who with undaunted toils
Sails unknown seas to unknown soils,
With various wonders feasts his sight:
What stranger wonders does he write!
5   We read, and in description view
Creatures which Adam never knew;
For, when we risque no contradiction,
It prompts the tongue to deal in fiction.
Those things that startle me or you,
10   I grant are strange; yet may be true.
Who doubts that elephants are found
For science and for sense renown'd?
Borri records their strength of parts,
Extent of thought, and skill in arts;
15   How they perform the law's decrees,
And save the state the hang-man's fees,
And how by travel understand
The language of another land.
Let those, who question this report,
20   To Pliny's ancient page resort.
How learn'd was that sagacious breed!
Who now (like them) the Greek can read!

    As one of these, in days of yore,
Rummag'd a shop of learning o'er,
25   Not like our modern dealers, minding
Only the margin's breadth and binding;
A book his curious eye detains,
Where, with exactest care and pains,
Were ev'ry beast and bird portray'd,
30   That e'er the search of man survey'd.
Their natures and their powers were writ
With all the pride of human wit;

The page he with attention spread,
And thus remark'd on what he read.
35   Man with strong reason is endow'd;
A Beast scarce instinct is allow'd:
But let this author's worth be try'd,
'Tis plain that neither was his guide.
Can he discern the diff'rent natures,
40 And weigh the pow'r of other creatures,
Who by the partial work hath shown
He knows so little of his own?
How falsely is the spaniel drawn!
Did man from him first learn to fawn?
45 A dog proficient in the trade!
He, the chief flatt'rer nature made!
Go, man, the ways of courts discern,
You'll find a spaniel still might learn.
How can the foxe's theft and plunder
50 Provoke his censure, or his wonder?
From courtiers tricks, and lawyers arts
The fox might well improve his parts.
The lyon, wolf, and tyger's brood
He curses, for their thirst of blood;
55 But is not man to man a prey?
Beasts kill for hunger, men for pay.
     The Bookseller, who heard him speak,
And saw him turn a page of Greek,
Thought, what a genius have I found!
60 Then thus addrest with bow profound.
     Learn'd Sir, if you'd employ your pen
Against the senseless sons of men,
Or write the history of Siam,
No man is better pay than I am;
65 Or, since you're learn'd in Greek, let's see
Something against the Trinity.
     When wrinkling with a sneer his trunk,
Friend, quoth the Elephant, you're drunk;
E'en keep your money, and be wise;

70   Leave man on man to criticise,
      For that you ne'er can want a pen
      Among the senseless sons of men,
      They unprovok'd will court the fray,
      Envy's a sharper spur than pay,
75   No author ever spar'd a brother,
      Wits are game-cocks to one another.

FABLE XXIV
The Butterfly and the Snail

    All upstarts, insolent in place,
    Remind us of their vulgar race.

    As, in the sun-shine of the morn,
    A Butterfly (but newly born)
5   Sate proudly perking on a rose;
      With pert conceit his bosom glows,
      His wings (all glorious to behold)
      Bedropt with azure, jet and gold,
      Wide he displays; the spangled dew
10   Reflects his eyes and various hue.
      His now forgotten friend, a Snail,
      Beneath his house, with slimy trail
      Crawles o'er the grass; whom when he spys,
      In wrath he to the gard'ner crys:
15   What means yon peasant's daily toil,
      From choaking weeds to rid the soil?
      Why wake you to the morning's care?
      Why with new arts correct the year?
      Why glows the peach with crimson hue?
20   And why the plum's inviting blue?
      Were they to feast his taste design'd,
      That vermine of voracious kind?
      Crush then the slow, the pilfring race,
      So purge thy garden from disgrace.

25   What arrogance! the Snail reply'd;
       How insolent is upstart pride!
       Hadst thou not thus, with insult vain,
       Provok'd my patience to complain;
       I had conceal'd thy meaner birth,
30   Nor trac'd thee to the scum of earth.
       For scarce nine suns have wak'd the hours,
       To swell the fruit and paint the flowers,
       Since I thy humbler life survey'd,
       In base, in sordid guise array'd;
35   A hideous insect, vile, unclean,
       You dragg'd a slow and noisome train,
       And from your spider bowels drew
       Foul film, and spun the dirty clue.
       I own my humble life, good friend;
40   Snail was I born, and snail shall end.
       And what's a butterfly? At best,
       He's but a caterpillar, drest:
       And all thy race (a num'rous seed)
       Shall prove of caterpillar breed.

FABLE XXIX
The Fox at the point of death

      A Fox, in life's extream decay,
      Weak, sick and faint, expiring lay;
      All appetite had left his maw,
      And age disarm'd his mumbling jaw.
5   His num'rous race around him stand
      To learn their dying sire's command;
      He rais'd his head with whining moan,
      And thus was heard the feeble tone.
      Ah sons, from evil ways depart,
10   My crimes lye heavy on my heart.

See, see, the murder'd geese appear!
Why are those bleeding turkeys there?
Why all around this cackling train,
Who haunt my ears for chicken slain?
15 The hungry foxes round them star'd,
And for the promis'd feast prepar'd.
  Where, Sir, is all this dainty cheer?
Nor turkey, goose, nor hen is here:
These are the phantoms of your brain,
20 And your sons lick their lips in vain.
  O gluttons, says the drooping sire;
Restrain inordinate desire;
Your liqu'rish taste you shall deplore,
When peace of conscience is no more.
25 Does not the hound betray our pace,
And gins and guns destroy our race?
Thieves dread the searching eye of power,
And never feel the quiet hour.
  Old-age, (which few of us shall know)
30 Now puts a period to my woe.
Would you true happiness attain,
Let honesty your passions rein;
So live in credit and esteem,
And, the good-name you lost, redeem.
35 The counsel's good, a fox replies,
Could we perform what you advise.
Think, what our ancestors have done;
A line of thieves from son to son;
To us descends the long disgrace,
40 And infamy hath mark'd our race.
Though we, like harmless sheep, should feed,
Honest in thought, in word, and deed,
Whatever hen-roost is decreas'd,
We shall be thought to share the feast.
45 The change shall never be believ'd,
A lost good-name is ne'er retriev'd.

Nay then, replys the feeble Fox,
(But, hark! I hear a hen that clocks)
Go, but be mod'rate in your food;
A chicken too might do me good.

FABLE XXXIX
The Father and Jupiter

The Man to Jove his suit preferr'd;
He begg'd a wife; his prayer was heard.
Jove wonder'd at his bold addressing.
For how precarious is the blessing!
5   A wife he takes. And now for heirs
Again he worries heav'n with prayers.
Jove nods assent. Two hopeful boys
And a fine girle reward his joys.
    Now more solicitous he grew,
10   And set their future lives in view;
He saw that all respect and duty
Were paid to wealth, to power, and beauty.
    Once more, he cries, accept my prayer,
Make my lov'd progeny thy care:
15   Let my first hope, my fav'rite boy,
All fortune's richest gifts enjoy.
My next with strong ambition fire,
May favour teach him to aspire,
'Till he the step of power ascend,
20   And courtiers to their idol bend.
With ev'ry grace, with ev'ry charm
My daughter's perfect features arm.
If Heav'n approve, a father's blest.
Jove smiles, and grants his full request.
25   The first, a miser at the heart,
Studious of ev'ry griping art,
Heaps hoards on hoards with anxious pain,
And all his life devotes to gain.

He feels no joy, his cares encrease,
30   He neither wakes nor sleeps in peace,
In fancy'd want, (a wretch compleat)
He starves, and yet he dares not eat.
    The next to sudden honours grew,
The thriving art of courts he knew;
35   He reach'd the height of power and place,
Then fell, the victim of disgrace.
    Beauty with early bloom supplies
His daughter's cheek, and points her eyes:
The vain coquette each suit disdains,
40   And glories in her lovers pains.
With age she fades, each lover flies,
Contemn'd, forlorn, she pines and dies.
    When Jove the father's grief survey'd,
And heard him Heav'n and Fate upbraid,
45   Thus spoke the God. By outward show
Men judge of happiness and woe:
Shall ignorance of good and ill
Dare to direct th'eternal will?
Seek virtue; and of that possest,
50   To Providence resign the rest.

FABLE XL
The two Monkeys

    The learned, full of inward pride,
The fops of outward show deride;
The fop, with learning at defiance,
Scoffs at the pedant and the science:
5   The Don, a formal, solemn strutter,
Despises Monsieur's airs and flutter;
While Monsieur mocks the formal fool,
Who looks, and speaks, and walks by rule.
Britain, a medly of the twain,
10   As pert as France, as grave as Spain,

In fancy wiser than the rest,
Laughs at them both, of both the jest.
Is not the poet's chiming close
Censur'd, by all the sons of prose?
15 While bards of quick imagination
Despise the sleepy prose narration.
Men laugh at apes, they men contemn;
For what are we, but apes to them?

    Two Monkeys went to Southwark fair,
20 No criticks had a sourer air.
They forc'd their way through draggled folks,
Who gap'd to catch Jack-Pudding's jokes.
Then took their tickets for the show,
And got by chance the foremost row.
25   To see their grave observing face
Provok'd a laugh thro' all the place.
    Brother, says Pug, and turn'd his head,
The rabble's monstrously ill-bred.
    Now through the booth loud hisses ran;
30 Nor ended 'till the Show began.
The tumbler whirles the flip-flap round,
With sommersets he shakes the ground;
The cord beneath the dancer springs;
Aloft in air the vaulter swings,
35 Distorted now, now prone depends,
Now through his twisted arms ascends;
The croud, in wonder and delight,
With clapping hands applaud the sight.
    With smiles, quoth Pug; If pranks like these
40 The giant apes of reason please,
How would they wonder at our arts!
They must adore us for our parts.
High on the twig I've seen you cling,
Play, twist and turn in airy ring;
45 How can those clumsy things, like me,
Fly with a bound from tree to tree?

But yet, by this applause, we find
These emulators of our kind
Discern our worth, our parts regard,
50   Who our mean mimicks thus reward.
      Brother, the grinning mate replies,
In this I grant that man is wise,
While good example they pursue,
We must allow some praise is due;
55   But when they strain beyond their guide,
I laugh to scorn the mimic pride.
For how fantastick is the sight,
To meet men always bolt upright,
Because we sometimes walk on two!
60   I hate the imitating crew.

FABLE XLII
The Jugglers

      A Juggler long through all the town
Had rais'd his fortune and renown;
You'd think (so far his art transcends)
The devil at his finger's ends.
5   Vice heard his fame, she read his bill;
Convinc'd of his inferior skill,
She sought his booth, and from the croud
Defy'd the man of art aloud.
      Is this then he so fam'd for slight,
10   Can this slow bungler cheat your sight,
Dares he with me dispute the prize?
I leave it to impartial eyes.
      Provok'd, the Juggler cry'd, 'tis done.
In science I submit to none.
15   Thus said. The cups and balls he play'd;
By turns, this here, that there, convey'd:
The cards, obedient to his words,
Are by a fillip turn'd to birds;

His little boxes change the grain,
20 Trick after trick deludes the train.
He shakes his bag, he shows all fair,
His fingers spread, and nothing there,
Then bids it rain with showers of gold,
And now his iv'ry eggs are told,
25 But when from thence the hen he draws,
Amaz'd spectators humm applause.
    Vice now stept forth and took the place,
With all the forms of his grimace.
    This magick looking-glass, she cries,
30 (There, hand it round) will charm your eyes:
Each eager eye the sight desir'd,
And ev'ry man himself admir'd.
    Next, to a senator addressing;
See this Bank-note; observe the blessing:
35 Breathe on the bill. Heigh, pass! 'Tis gone.
Upon his lips a padlock shone.
A second puff the magick broke,
The padlock vanish'd, and he spoke.
    Twelve bottles rang'd upon the board,
40 All full, with heady liquor stor'd,
By clean conveyance disappear,
And now two bloody swords are there.
    A purse she to a thief expos'd;
At once his ready fingers clos'd:
45 He opes his fist, the treasure's fled,
He sees a halter in its stead.
    She bids Ambition hold a wand,
He grasps a hatchet in his hand.
    A box of charity she shows:
50 Blow here; and a church-warden blows,
'Tis vanish'd with conveyance neat,
And on the table smoaks a treat.
    She shakes the dice, the board she knocks,
And from all pockets fills her box.
55   She next a meagre rake addrest;

This picture see; her shape, her breast!
What youth, and what inviting eyes!
Hold her, and have her. With surprise,
His hand expos'd a box of pills;
60   And a loud laugh proclaim'd his ills.
     A counter, in a miser's hand,
Grew twenty guineas at command;
She bids his heir the summ retain,
And 'tis a counter now again.
65   A guinea with her touch you see
Take ev'ry shape but Charity;
And not one thing, you saw, or drew,
But chang'd from what was first in view.
     The Juggler now, in grief of heart,
70   With this submission own'd her art.
Can I such matchless slight withstand?
How practice hath improv'd your hand!
But now and then I cheat the throng;
You ev'ry day, and all day long.

FABLE L
The Hare and many Friends

    Friendship, like love, is but a name,
Unless to one you stint the flame.
The child, whom many fathers share,
Hath seldom known a father's care;
'Tis thus in friendships; who depend
On many, rarely find a friend.

    A Hare, who, in a civil way,
Comply'd with ev'ry thing, like Gay,
Was known by all the bestial train,
10   Who haunt the wood, or graze the plain:
    Her care was, never to offend,
And ev'ry creature was her friend.

As forth she went at early dawn
To taste the dew-besprinkled lawn,
15 Behind she hears the hunter's cries,
And from the deep-mouth'd thunder flies;
She starts, she stops, she pants for breath,
She hears the near advance of death,
She doubles, to mis-lead the hound,
20 And measures back her mazy round;
'Till, fainting in the publick way,
Half dead with fear she gasping lay.
    What transport in her bosom grew,
When first the horse appear'd in view!
25   Let me, says she, your back ascend,
And owe my safety to a friend,
You know my feet betray my flight,
To friendship ev'ry burthen's light.
    The horse reply'd, poor honest puss,
30 It grieves my heart to see thee thus;
Be comforted, relief is near;
For all your friends are in the rear.
    She next the stately bull implor'd;
And thus reply'd the mighty lord.
35 Since ev'ry beast alive can tell
That I sincerely wish you well,
I may, without offence, pretend
To take the freedom of a friend;
Love calls me hence; a fav'rite cow
40 Expects me near yon barley mow:
And when a lady's in the case,
You know, all other things give place.
To leave you thus might seem unkind;
But see, the goat is just behind.
45   The goat remark'd her pulse was high,
Her languid head, her heavy eye;
My back, says he, may do you harm;
The sheep's at hand, and wool is warm.
    The sheep was feeble, and complain'd,

50 His sides a load of wool sustain'd,
    Said he was slow, confest his fears;
    For hounds eat sheep as well as hares.
        She now the trotting calf addrest,
    To save from death a friend distrest.
55   Shall I, says he, of tender age,
    In this important care engage?
    Older and abler past you by;
    How strong are those! how weak am I!
    Should I presume to bear you hence,
60 Those friends of mine may take offence.
    Excuse me then. You know my heart.
    But dearest friends, alas, must part!
    How shall we all lament! Adieu.
    For see the hounds are just in view.

FABLES, 1738

FABLE I
The Dog and the Fox

To a Lawyer
    I know you Lawyers can, with ease,
    Twist words and meanings as you please;
    That language, by your skill made pliant,
    Will bend to favour ev'ry client;
5   That 'tis the fee directs the sense
    To make out either side's pretense.
    When you peruse the clearest case,
    You see it with a double face;
    For scepticism's your profession;
10 You hold there's doubt in all expression.
        Hence is the bar with fees supply'd,
    Hence eloquence takes either side:
    Your hand would have but paultry gleaning,

Cou'd ev'ry man express his meaning.
15 Who dares presume to pen a deed,
Unless you previously are fee'd?
'Tis drawn; and, to augment the cost,
In dull prolixity engrost:
And now we're well secur'd by law,
20 Till the next brother find a flaw.
 Read o'er a will. Was't ever known,
But you could make the will your own?
For when you read, 'tis with intent
To find out meanings never meant.
25 Since things are thus, se defendendo,
I bar fallacious innuendo.
 Sagacious Porta's skill could trace
Some beast or bird in ev'ry face;
The head, the eye, the nose's shape,
30 Prov'd this an owl, and that an ape.
When, in the sketches thus design'd,
Resemblance brings some friend to mind;
You show the piece, and give the hint,
And find each feature in the print;
35 So monstrous like the portrait's found,
All know it and the laugh goes round.
Like him I draw from gen'ral nature:
Is't I or you then fix the satire?
 So, Sir, I beg you spare your pains
40 In making comments on my strains:
All private slander I detest,
I judge not of my neighbour's breast;
Party and prejudice I hate,
And write no libels on the state.
45 Shall not my fable censure vice,
Because a knave is over-nice?
And, lest the guilty hear and dread,
Shall not the Decalogue be read?
If I lash vice in gen'ral fiction,
50 Is't I apply or self-conviction?

Brutes are my theme. Am I to blame,
If men in morals are the same?
I no man call or ape or ass;
'Tis his own conscience holds the glass.
55   Thus void of all offence I write:
Who claims the fable, knows his right.

A shepherd's Dog, unskill'd in sports,
Pick'd up acquaintance of all sorts:
Among the rest a Fox he knew;
60   By frequent chat their friendship grew.
Says Renard, 'tis a cruel case,
That man should stigmatize our race.
No doubt, among us rogues you find,
As among dogs and human kind;
65   And yet (unknown to me and you)
There may be honest men and true.
Thus slander tries, whate'er it can,
To put us on the foot with man.
Let my own actions recommend;
70   No prejudice can blind a friend:
You know me free from all disguise;
My honour as my life I prize.
By talk like this from all mistrust
The Dog was cur'd, and thought him just.
75   As on a time the Fox held forth
On conscience, honesty, and worth,
Sudden he stopt; he cock'd his ear;
Low dropt his brushy tail with fear.
Bless us! the hunters are abroad.
80   What's all that chatter on the road?
Hold, says the Dog, we're safe from harm:
'Twas nothing but a false alarm.
At yonder town 'tis market day;
Some farmer's wife is on the way:
85   'Tis so, (I know her pye-ball'd mare)
Dame Dobbins with her poultry-ware.

Renard grew huff. Says he, This sneer
From you I little thought to hear;
Your meaning in your looks I see.
90 Pray what's dame Dobbins, friend, to me?
Did I e'er make her poultry thinner?
Prove that I owe the dame a dinner.
  Friend, quoth the Cur, I meant no harm:
Then why so captious? Why so warm?
95 My words, in common acceptation,
Could never give this provocation.
No lamb (for ought I ever knew)
May be more innocent than you.
  At this, gall'd Renard winc'd and swore
100 Such language ne'er was giv'n before.
  What's lamb to me? This saucy hint
Shows me, base knave, which way you squint.
If t'other night your master lost
Three lambs; am I to pay the cost?
105 Your vile reflections would imply
That I'm the thief. You dog, you lye.
  Thou knave, thou fool, (the Dog reply'd)
The name is just, take either side;
Thy guilt these applications speak:
110 Sirrah, 'tis conscience makes you squeak.
  So saying, on the Fox he flies.
The self-convicted felon dies.

FABLE II
The Vultur, the Sparrow, and other Birds

To a Friend in the Country
lines 1-72
  E'er I begin, I must premise
Our ministers are good and wise;
So, though malicious tongues apply,
Pray, what care they, or what care I?

5   If I am free with courts; be't known,
       I ne'er presume to mean our own.
       If gen'ral morals seem to joke
       On ministers and such like folk,
       A captious fool may take offence;
10   What then? He knows his own pretence.
       I meddle with no state-affairs,
       But spare my jest to save my ears.
       Our present schemes are too profound
       For Machiavel himself to sound:
15   To censure 'em I've no pretension;
       I own they're past my comprehension.
           You say your brother wants a place,
       ('Tis many a younger brother's case)
       And that he very soon intends
20   To ply the court and teaze his friends.
       If there his merits chance to find
       A patriot of an open mind,
       Whose constant actions prove him just
       To both a king's and people's trust,
25   May he, with gratitude, attend,
       And owe his rise to such a friend.
           You praise his parts for bus'ness fit,
       His learning, probity, and wit;
       But those alone will never do,
30   Unless his patron have 'em too.
           I've heard of times, (pray God defend us,
       We're not so good but he can mend us)
       When wicked ministers have trod
       On kings and people, law and God;
35   With arrogance they girt the throne,
       And knew no int'rest but their own.
       Then virtue, from preferment barr'd,
       Gets nothing but its own reward.
       A gang of petty knaves attend 'em,
40   With proper parts to recommend 'em.
       Then, if his patron burn with lust,

The first in favour's pimp the first.
His doors are never clos'd to spies,
Who chear his heart with double lyes;
45 They flatter him, his foes defame,
So lull the pangs of guilt and shame.
If schemes of lucre haunt his brain,
Projectors swell his greedy train;
Vile brokers ply his private ear
50 With jobs of plunder for the year.
All consciences must bend and ply;
You must vote on, and not know why:
Through thick and thin you must go on;
One scruple, and your place is gone.
55   Since plagues like these have curst a land,
And fav'rites cannot always stand,
Good courtiers should for change be ready,
And not have principles too steady;
For should a knave engross the pow'r,
60 (God shield the realm from that sad hour)
He must have rogues or slavish fools;
For what's a knave without his tools?
    Wherever those a people drain,
And strut with infamy and gain,
65 I envy not their guilt and state,
And scorn to share the public hate.
Let their own servile creatures rise,
By screening fraud and venting lyes:
Give me, kind heav'n, *a private station,
70 A mind serene for contemplation,
Title and profit I resign,
The post of honour shall be mine.

* — *When impious men bear sway,*
  The post of honour is a private station.
                              ADDISON. [Gay]

FABLE XVI
The Ravens, the Sexton, and the Earth-Worm

To Laura
lines 73-158

  Beneath a venerable yew,
That in the lonely church-yard grew,
75 Two Ravens sate. In solemn croak
Thus one his hungry friend bespoke.
  Methinks I scent some rich repast,
The savour strengthens with the blast;
Snuff then; the promis'd feast inhale,
80 I taste the carcase in the gale.
Near yonder trees the farmer's steed,
From toil and ev'ry drudg'ry freed,
Hath groan'd his last. A dainty treat!
To birds of taste delicious meat!
85 A Sexton, busy at his trade,
To hear their chat suspends his spade:
Death struck him with no farther thought,
Than merely as the fees he brought.
Was ever two such blund'ring fowls,
90 In brains and manners less than owls!
Blockheads, says he, learn more respect.
Know ye on whom ye thus reflect?
In this same grave (who does me right,
Must own the work is strong and tight)
95 The squire, that yon fair hall possest,
To night shall lay his bones at rest.
Whence could the gross mistake proceed?
The squire was somewhat fat indeed.
What then? the meanest bird of prey
100 Such want of sense could ne'er betray;
For sure some diff'rence must be found
(Suppose the smelling organ sound)
In carcases, (say what you can)
Or where's the dignity of man?

105   With due respect to human race
        The Ravens undertook the case.
        In such similitude of scent,
        Man ne'er could think reflection meant.
        As Epicures extol a treat,
110   And seem their sav'ry words to eat,
        They prais'd dead horse, luxurious food,
        The ven'son of the prescient brood.
        The Sexton's indignation mov'd,
        The mean comparison reprov'd;
115   Their undiscerning palate blam'd,
        Which two-legg'd carrion thus defam'd.
        Reproachful speech from either side
        The want of argument supply'd.
        They rail, revile. As often ends
120   The contest of disputing friends.
        Hold, says the fowl; since human pride
        With confutation ne'er comply'd,
        Let's state the case, and then refer
        The knotty point: For taste may err.
125   As thus he spoke, from out the mold
        An Earth-worm, huge of size, unroll'd
        His monstrous length. They strait agree
        To chuse him as their referee.
        So to th'experience of his jaws
130   Each states the merits of the cause.
        He paus'd, and with a solemn tone
        Thus made his sage opinion known.
        On carcases of ev'ry kind
        This maw hath elegantly din'd;
135   Provok'd by luxury or need,
        On beast or fowl or man I feed:
        Such small distinction's in the savour,
        By turns I chuse the fancy'd flavour;
        Yet I must own (that human beast)
140   A glutton is the rankest feast.
        Man, cease this boast; for human pride

Hath various tracts to range beside.
The prince who kept the world in awe,
The judge whose dictate fix'd the law,
145 The rich, the poor, the great, the small,
Are levell'd. Death confounds 'em all.
Then think not that we reptiles share
Such cates, such elegance of fare;
The only true and real good
150 Of man was never vermine's food.
'Tis seated in th' immortal mind;
Virtue distinguishes mankind,
And that (as yet ne'er harbour'd here)
Mounts with the soul we know not where.
155 So good-man Sexton, since the case
Appears with such a dubious face,
To neither I the cause determine,
For diff'rent tastes please diff'rent vermine.

MY OWN EPITAPH
[*Poems on Several Occasions*, 1720]

Life is a jest; and all things show it,
I thought so once; but now I know it.

NOTES

These notes are inevitably brief. The serious student will consult the comprehensive Commentary of the Dearing-Beckwith edition.

WINE line 25 Xantippe] wife of Socrates, traditionally a type of bad temper. line 31 Branched Crew] the image is of cuckoldry. line 152 Jocund and Boon] cf. *Paradise Lost* 9.793. line 157 Melampus] one of Actaeon's hounds. Ovid, *Metamorphoses* 3.206. line 276 Lib'ral Hand] cf. *Paradise Lost* 9.997.

SHEPHERD'S WEEK
'Monday' line 92 White-pot] a kind of custard or milk-pudding. line 99 Hot-Cockles] 'a rustic game in which one player lay face downwards, or knelt down with his eyes covered, and being struck on the back by the others in turn, guessed who struck him'. *OED.*
'Wednesday' lines 9ff. The ears, the 'homely Guise', and 'New-Market', perhaps suggest an alternative way of reading 'D- - -y'. Lines 11-15 allude to songs and a farce (*Wonders in the Sun*, 1706) by D'Urfey.
'Saturday' line 56 Colworts] cabbages. line 87 Jack-pudding] a common name for a clown. Cf. *Fables* (1727) 40.22. line 109 *All in the Land of Essex*] the opening words of a broadside by John Denham. Gay's catalogue of popular songs and ballads parodies Virgil, *Eclogues* 6.41ff.

TRIVIA
I. 43ff. Doily] a cheap woollen material. Drugget] a thin cloth of wool, wool and silk or wool and linen. Camlet] a ribbed worsted. Roquelaure, Bavaroy] types of fashionable long cloaks. Surtout] a greatcoat. Kersey] a coarse woollen cloth. 203ff. Alecto] one of the Furies. The bathing fair surprised by Glaucus the sea-god was the nymph Scylla, transformed by Circe (Ovid, *Metamorphoses* 13.900-68, 14.1-74). 245ff. Mulciber] Vulcan. Paphian Spouse] Venus.

III. 4 Cynthia] a name for Diana, associated both with the goddess Trivia, and the moon. 85-86 *Iliad* 8.134ff. 95-96,

97-100   *Aeneid* 2.735ff., 9.367ff.   185 Ostrea] an oyster-girl.
334   supposedly the method by which the Carthaginians executed
their captive Regulus, after his refusal to negotiate peace on their
behalf with Rome. See Horace, *Odes* 3.5.   368 *Aeneid* 2.707ff.
377-78 See *Georgics* 1.463ff.   407ff. a parody of the classic poets'
vaunt (Ovid, *Metamorphoses* 15.871ff.; Horace, *Odes* 3.30.1;
cf. *Shepherd's Week,* 'Saturday' 117-18), followed by an account
of the uses to which unsold copies of the works of such third-rate
poets as Ward and Gildon might be put.

ECLOGUES
'The Birth of the Squire' line 14   October] beer brewed in
October.
'The Tea-Table' lines 21ff.   It was fashionable to dress as shep-
herds and shepherdesses at mask-balls. The green dress has sexual
connotations; cf. *Shepherd's Week,* 'Thursday' 135-36: 'He vows,
he swears, he'll give me a green Gown / Oh dear! I fall *adown,
adown, adown!'*   line 31 mob'd] hidden by a mob-cap.
line 67 the Park]   St. James's was notorious as a rendezvous for
sexual dalliance. See Rochester, 'A Ramble in St. James's Park';
Etherege, *The Man of Mode, passim*; and Gay's *Epistle III,* 'To the
Right Honourable William Pulteney Esq.', lines 127-130.
line 100   Ombre] a card game; see *The Rape of the Lock* 3.25ff.

FABLES (1727)
X. 13 Borri] Gay refers to *La Chiave del Gabinetto del Cavagliere
Gioseppe Francesco Borri* (1681).
XLII. 15 the cups and balls] the game of thimblerig.

FABLES (1738)
I. 25 se defendendo] in self-defence.   27 Porta] Giovanni
Battista della Porta, best known of the physiognomists, typed
human faces by animal models in his *De Humana Physiognoma*
(1586).
II. 12   save my ears] a reference to the penalty for seditious
libel, by Gay's time not in use.
XVI. 112 prescient brood] ravens were proverbially prophetic.